The Golden Voices of Baseball

BY TED PATTERSON

Foreword by Curt Gowdy

The Golden Voices of Baseball

By Ted Patterson
Foreword by Curt Gowdy

Sports Publishing L.L.C.
Publisher: **Peter L. Bannon**
Senior Managing Editors: **Joseph J. Bannon, Jr. and Susan M. Moyer**
Art Director: **K. Jeffrey Higgerson**

Graphic Designer: **Christine Mohrbacher**
Acquisition Editor: **Mike Pearson**
Developmental Editors: **Stephanie Fuqua and Scott Rauguth**
Copy Editor: **Cynthia L. McNew**

Front cover photo:
**Provided by National Baseball Hall of Fame Library,
Cooperstown, N.Y.**
Back cover photo: **From the author's collection**

ISBN: 1-58261-498-9

Table of Contents

GOLDEN VOICES TRACKS CD 1

Announcer	Track #
Introduction by Curt Gowdy	
Harold Arlin	2-3
Tom "Red" Manning	4-6
Ty Tyson	7-8
Bob Elson	9-12
Quin Ryan	13
Ted Husing	14
France Laux	15-17
Pat Flanagan	18
Bill Stern	19-22
Stan Lomax	23
Mel Allen	24
Jack Graney	25-26
Jimmy Dudley	27-29
Al Helfer	30-31
Bob Prince	32, 35-36
Rosey Rowswell	33-34
Byrum Saam	37-38
Gene Kelly	39-40
Jack Brickhouse	41-42
Lindsey Nelson	43-45

GOLDEN VOICES TRACKS CD 2

Announcer	Track #
Russ Hodges	1-5
Dick Bray	6-8
Waite Hoyt	9
Harry Caray	10-11
Jack Buck	12
Curt Gowdy	13-15
Vin Scully	16, 18-20
Connie Desmond	17
Red Barber	21-23
Halsey Hall	24-25
Bob Wolff	26-27
Chuck Thompson	28-29
Buddy Blattner	30
Dizzy Dean	31-32
Jim Woods	33-34
Jim Britt	35-37
Vince Lloyd	38-40
Ernie Harwell	41-45
Connie Desmond	46-48

Dedication

To the sportscasting pioneers, the trailblazers of radio's yesteryear, who began with the basic rudiments and evolved a craft that became a profession. Each and every one of you was a true golden voice of baseball.

Foreword

By Curt Gowdy

 Curt Gowdy Introduction: CD 1: Track 1

It was back in the summer of 1968 that I first met Ted Patterson. He journeyed all the way to my Lawrence, Mass. radio station to interview me about my career as a play-by-play sportscaster. As it turned out, Ted was traveling all over the country interviewing both the pioneer and present-day announcers. He had discovered that very little had been written about the men and the profession of sports broadcasting. Three years later, after his military career and strictly through happenstance, Ted would end up working for me, helping to assemble my daily NBC radio show. A few years later, he was off to WBAL in Baltimore to launch his own sportscasting career.

More than three decades have gone by, and finally, Ted's research is being recognized in *The Golden Voices of Baseball.* The great announcers of the golden era are being chronicled not only through written text and with never-before-seen photographs, but also with their actual voices, through interviews and play-by-play highlights.

I'm proud to be one of the golden voices. It was an era before television, when the broadcasters painted a word picture. Even when I became the voice of NBC television sports, I still missed the intimacy and creativity of radio.

Many of my contemporaries have passed from the scene, but thanks to this book, they will live forever. Enjoy the memories.

Curt Gowdy, Ted Patterson and Ken Coleman at Fenway Park, 1971.

Preface

"Certainly it is a mystery still to me, this standing by a tiny instrument of wires and springs, talking in ordinary tones and realizing I am heard by millions of people from three feet to three thousand miles away. I know you are sitting in little farmhouses or in city apartments with head phones over your ears, standing by loudspeakers in the city streets, or massed in great concert halls, all listening to what we say in quiet syllables, just as if we were talking to our wives. Yet we never see that vast audience, your massed ranked faces, and you never see ours. We are voices out of the night, almost out of the unknown."

—Graham McNamee, pioneer sports broadcaster, 1926.

Graham McNamee helped lay the foundation of sportscasting, but it was the team of Jimmy Dudley and Jack Graney that drew my interest while I was growing up in the 1950s. Dudley and Graney broadcast the fortunes of the Cleveland Indians, and in 1954 the Indians were the biggest story in baseball. In my hometown of Mansfield, Ohio, the voices of Dudley and Graney could be heard in drugstores, taverns, and blaring out from the kitchen radio through almost every screen door on a hot summer's night. Happily, Jimmy Dudley joined the ranks of announcing immortals by being named the 1997 Ford Frick winner at the Baseball Hall of Fame.

By 1962, fascinated by the voices of the announcers, I was compiling highlight tapes on my friend Steve Sturges's bulky new tape recorder. We made our own documentaries, replete with Army-Navy games, NCAA basketball championships, and Jim Brown touchdown runs.

This sportscasting history is dedicated to men like Jimmy Dudley and Jack Graney, men who sat on a stool in a booth and served as the eyes and ears of the listener, painting a word-picture like an artist on canvas. During radio's heyday, the broadcasters were almost like members of the family. They were the link to the games, and many were so popular that they were given special days in their honor. When television took over for radio as the focal medium, the voices gave way to the images. One era gave way to another, but radio remains today, despite the proliferation of cable television, a key ingredient in the marketing and success of a team, whether it be pro or college.

My research began in 1966 while I was a student at the University of Dayton. I soon realized how little was known about the history of sports broadcasting. Radio and TV stations are notorious for disposing of historical records, which made my task a difficult one. That's why I elected to talk to the announcers themselves. Each contributed his own stories to complete a tapestry that wove through several decades. Most were up in age then and very few remain today.

Ironically, the very first sports announcer, Harold Arlin, resided just a block from my Ohio home. Others were scattered all over the country. All, with few exceptions, were amazingly cooperative. Along with Arlin, three others were particularly helpful: Dick Bray, who worked with Red Barber in Cincinnati; legendary fight broadcaster Sam Taub, who regaled me with stories and anecdotes about covering sports in New York City when Jack Johnson was heavyweight champion and John McGraw managed the Giants; and France Laux, the pioneer sports announcer on KMOX in St. Louis, who gave me some great personal photos and drove me to Bowling Green, Missouri, to interview Jack Graney. Hopefully, the Sam Taub story will be included in a future volume about the golden voices covering boxing and other sports.

Things did not always go smoothly in my pursuit of sportscasting history, especially for a college kid operating on a slim budget. While I was interviewing the widow of colorful Pittsburgh baseball broadcaster Rosey Rowswell, my car was being stolen outside her apartment near Forbes Field. Both Bill Stern and Howard Cosell treated me rudely in New York, but both eventually consented to interviews. I remember driving through riot-torn Detroit in 1967 to interview Harry Wismer in a Port Huron, Michigan, hospital.

Help was also provided by baseball historian Lee Allen of the Hall of Fame in Cooperstown and legendary baseball writer Fred Lieb, along with veteran *Dayton Daily News* sports editor Si Burick, all of whom are now deceased. I spent a wonderful two summers with Lee at the Hall of Fame. The following summer he passed away suddenly at age 54. Current Hall of Fame researchers Greg Harris and Jeremy Jones have taken over where Lee left off. A special thank you to WOR radio historian Jim Thibodeaux.

I would be remiss if I didn't thank the many folks who lodged me in different ports of call. College roommates Bob Gallo in Pittsburgh, Jim Brown in Utica, New York (near Cooperstown) and Tony Zirpoli in New York City and their families provided room, board and moral support as I made the rounds in quest of pioneer sportscasters.

While I was a grad student at Miami University in Ohio where my thesis became a series of 50 half-hour programs on the pioneer sportscasters, Kathy Porter was an invaluable help in organizing this project. Her typing and organizational skills alone were priceless. Several decades later, Michael Patterson has provided his computer knowledge to help a father from another era.

I'd like to thank producer-engineer John Vincent for his help in producing the CDs that accompany this book, featuring the actual golden voices of baseball. Recording equipment has changed dramatically over the years, and John was able to convert the old interviews and highlights into the technology of today.

Special thanks also goes to Mike Pearson, the acquisitions director at Sports Publishing L.L.C. Mike was excited about this project from the very beginning. He believed in it and eventually opened the doors for it to reach publication after many close calls, near misses and out-and-out refusals over a period of three decades. Sports Publishing staffers Scott Rauguth and Stephanie Fuqua helped develop the final product.

Appreciation goes out to my mentor and old boss Curt Gowdy for several reasons. First, his cooperation and interest in this project from the beginning. Second, the two years I worked directly for him, learning the arts of interviewing and writing and tapping his vast sportscasting legacy. And third and last, his participation in this project, both his written and spoken words.

Another legend, Ernie Harwell, was a solid source who has bridged the pioneer days to the present time. So many have departed the scene, but others like Ernie, Vin Scully, Bob Wolff, Les Keiter and Curt Gowdy are still with us. This book adds to their legacy and pays tribute to a unique fraternity of great voices, great wordsmiths and great characters.

Introduction

It was a whirlwind courtship, but the matchup was perfect, one that has lasted three quarters of a century and is still going strong—sports and radio. The early detractors, who objected to giving the public something for nothing, soon changed their thinking as vast new fan territories were created. From carrier pigeons to Morse code to actual transmission of the spoken word, radio turned tiny steps in communications into giant strides. In 1904, President Theodore Roosevelt exchanged pleasantries over a Massachusetts-based station created by radio pioneer Guglielmo Marconi, while in 1909 Arctic explorer Robert Peary radioed back to civilization, "I have found the pole." In 1910, famed tenor Enrico Caruso stood on the bare stage of the Metropolitan Opera in front of a crude microphone and belted out one of his famous arias. These were humble beginnings indeed.

On April 14, 1912, the young operator of a station atop the Wannamaker department store in New York, David Sarnoff, took the first message from the S.S. *Olympic*, 1,400 miles out at sea: "S.S. *Titanic* ran into iceberg. Sinking fast." For three days and three nights, Sarnoff, who would become a broadcasting giant with RCA and NBC, remained at his telegraph key relaying updates to reporters and concerned friends and relatives. Many historians say it was the birth of radio news.

World War I helped speed up radio's development, and by the early 1920s, several cities had commercially licensed stations. KDKA in Pittsburgh, the first licensed station, went on the air on Nov. 2, 1920, with the Harding-Cox election returns. WWJ in Detroit began at the same time, and in October 1921, WJZ began operating from a factory roof in Newark, New Jersey. Wattage was poor and rooftop antennas were propped up with clotheslines, but thousands flocked to buy radio sets. There were 30 stations by the end of 1921 and 200 by the end of 1922.

It was only a matter of time before the pioneer program directors, who began airing church services, political speeches and vaudeville sketches, discovered the vast realm of broadcasting live sporting events.

This book tells the story of those early days through the eyes of the men who pioneered the sportscasting profession. Their recollections, mixed with historical overview and hundreds of remarkable, many never before seen photographs, trace the industry from its humble beginnings to the billion-dollar rights fees of today. The majority of the pioneer announcers, Harold Arlin, Tom Manning, France Laux, Ty Tyson, Mel Allen, Bob Prince, Harry Wismer, Rosey Rowswell, Bill Stern, Jack Graney, Bob Elson, Al Helfer, Russ Hodges, Connie Desmond and so many others, are gone

David Sarnoff, a wireless operator, is credited with the birth of radio news after he remained at the telegraph for three days after the Titanic disaster, relaying news updates to reporters and concerned friends and relatives.

now. They were interviewed back in the mid-to-late 1960s and early 1970s when many were already retired and in their 70s and 80s. Others had been around for decades and were in the twilight of their careers. They shared many things in common, including a zest to tell their stories of what it was like covering and broadcasting some of the legendary events of sports history.

Not only will you be able to read about the great sportscasters in history and view some remarkable photographs of their careers, but you'll also be able to hear their actual voices and memorable broadcasts in a specially produced CD set.

These men, indeed, were the "Golden Voices of Baseball." Turn on your radio, set your dial, sit back, and let the games begin.

One of radio's most famous broadcasts was November 2, 1920, when KDKA in Pittsburgh opened a new era in communications by announcing the returns from the Harding-Cox presidential election.

WGN's first studio, at the Drake Hotel in Chicago in 1924. Curtains functioned as sound deadeners, and the wind-up phonograph on the right was probably radio's first disc-jockey turntable.

Dr. Frank Conrad conducted the experimental work that led to the establishment of KDKA, and he also supervised the construction of the station.

This 1923 advertising photo was designed to draw listeners to KDKA's broadcasts.

VOICES IN THE AIR: THE EARLY YEARS

Right off the bat, there is conjecture on who actually broadcast the first sporting event on radio. Although KDKA in Pittsburgh claims the official distinction, there are those who say different. Way back in the fall of 1912, an attempt was made to broadcast football games using a spark transmitter and regular telegraph signals by the University of Minnesota's experimental radio station. In October 1920, station 8MK in Detroit (later WWJ) was broadcasting summaries of the World Series between Cleveland and Brooklyn, but these consisted primarily of just the final scores.

Sports broadcasting officially debuted on the night of April 11, 1921, in the Pittsburgh Motor Garden, when Florent Gibson, the sports editor of the *Pittsburgh Post*, broadcast the blow-by-blow of a featherweight match between Johnny "Hutch" Ray and Johnny Dundee. Ray won the fight, though Dundee would go on to capture the featherweight championship of the world on July 26, 1923.

The headline in the Tuesday morning *Post* read: "Johnny Ray Defeats Dundee in Brilliant Battle—Scotch Wop Both Outboxed and Outfought by Local Boy in Ten Thrilling Sessions." Below the headline, in a separate box, was another story: "Wireless Journalism Takes Boxing Fans Up to the Ringside." The article described how "wireless telephone from ringside to the *Post* enabled a news extra to be on the street with a full account of the fight a few minutes after the decision was given to Ray. More than 40,000 wireless telephone operators from Dallas to Montreal and Montana to Maine heard the sporting editor of the *Post* as he dictated the action of the ring battle he was witnessing. The *Post* scored a news triumph all over the continent." There was also a note that the city of Hartford, Connecticut heard the encounter:

"all the sounds of the conflict, the clang of the gong, and the shouts of the fans."

Gibson, who in 1970 at the age of 82 was still working on the copy desk of the *Post*, remembered "the blood and water from the ring splashing all over me. An old-fashioned phone served as the microphone." Gibson thus got credit for being the first sportscaster. The West Virginia native played college football at Dennison University in Ohio and joined the *Post* in 1912. He was still there 58 years later, long after the Pittsburgh Motor Garden had been transformed into a Cadillac agency. Gibson was somewhat of a combatant himself, having wrestled in a Pittsburgh burlesque house during his lunch hours under the name "The Masked Marvel."

Gibson's claim to fame as the first sportscaster has been passed over by many, as it was generally believed that the Jack Dempsey-Georges Carpentier heavyweight title fight at Boyles's Thirty Acres in Hoboken, New Jersey on July 2, 1921, was the first fight broadcast. David Sarnoff had gone to J. Andrew White, the editor of *Wireless Age* magazine, with the idea of broadcasting the fight nationwide. Since they had no radio station, they decided to construct their own. The Delaware, Lackawanna and Western Railway let them string their aerial wires on the railway's great steel tower, which was eight miles from ringside. The transmitter, borrowed from the navy with the help of Assistant Secretary of the Navy Franklin D. Roosevelt, was housed on a railroad car.

Dempsey decked the smaller challenger twice, administering a terrific beating to the "Orchid Man" from France. White, with Sarnoff at his side, could only hope that his colorful description was being heard. In fact, some 300,000 people in clubs, halls, theaters and homes heard the

The author (left) with Florence Gibson in 1968. Gibson may have been the first sports announcer, as he broadcast a boxing match on April 11, 1921.

Harold Arlin in 1922.

broadcast from as far as 500 miles away. One ship reported hearing the fight 400 miles out at sea.

The news of what a Reuters official called the "world's first real broadcast" was reported throughout Europe. A new era of communication had been ushered in. Wrote White afterwards: "With bedlam breaking loose on every side, it's a wonder it sounded even intelligible. The men punched quicker than could be noted by speech. Their speed baffled the tongue; even the eye was strained. I could only give the punches that did some damage. Can't help liking Dempsey. He's not very pretty but he's a clean sportsman. You could see it in his eyes on the first knockdown that he didn't want to hit him again. This brute strength business that everyone talks about is all poppycock. And nothing could be more naive and natural than the way Jack sprang forward at the final ten and lifted up his gallant opponent in his arms."

💿 Harold Arlin: CD 1: Tracks 2, 3

Back in Pittsburgh, the Westinghouse-owned KDKA, the brainchild of experimenter Frank Conrad, was beginning to rack up several firsts. In early August 1921, Harold Arlin, a Westinghouse foreman loaned to the radio station in January as the medium's first full-time announcer, broadcast the Davis Cup tennis matches between the British Isles and Australia from the Allegheny Country Club. On August 5, 1921, Arlin broadcast the first major-league baseball game as the Pirates defeated the Phillies at Forbes Field by a score of 8 to 5. The game was delayed for 30 minutes because Charley Grimm of the Pirates was hit by a pitch and rushed to the hospital.

Arlin had stumbled into radio quite by accident. The station was on the roof of the Westinghouse factory, and Arlin had gone up out of curiosity, auditioned for the announcing job, and to his amazement, got it.

A native of LaHarp, Illinois, Arlin moved to Carthage, Missouri with his family in 1900 when he was five years old. After graduating from the University of Kansas as an electrical engineer in 1917, Arlin joined Westinghouse in Pittsburgh. At Kansas, his gym instructor was another pioneer, Dr. Charles Naismith, the father of basketball. Arlin had always had the ambition to return to Missouri and farm, but it never happened. "I'd planted 20 acres of wheat and plowed 35 acres of soil three times before I left for Pittsburgh. I never got back to the harvest."

Instead he found himself wearing a tuxedo and broadcasting dance band remotes. "We always wore tuxedos because of all the prominent people we met and interviewed," he recalled. Remote broadcasting became an integral part of the format and in the five years he was with KDKA, the station broadcast from 65 different locations, including hotels, theaters and country clubs. Arlin was quickly becoming a popular figure. "Kindly tell your announcer, the gentleman who gives the baseball scores at night," wrote a housewife from Quebec, Canada, "that I have four boys who listen to him every night. His pronunciation is so perfect that even though they speak French, they can still understand him." The *London Times* called Arlin, "The best known American voice in Europe."

It was only a matter of time before sports entered the KDKA broadcast schedule. Besides live events, Arlin also conducted interviews with well known celebrities of the time, including Will Rogers and Babe Ruth. "The Yankees were playing an exhibition game in Pittsburgh," remembered Arlin, "and since it was the first time the Babe appeared on radio, a short speech was written for him to read. When I introduced him, he suddenly came down with an awful case of mike fright. Sensing the trouble, I reached over and grabbed his speech and read it in the manner Babe might deliver it. In the meantime, the Babe composed himself somewhat and lit up a cigar. I soon received several letters expounding on what a wonderful voice Babe Ruth had."

On October 8, 1921, KDKA, seizing upon the intense interest in Pitt football, sent Arlin and an engineer out to

Harold Arlin guests with Bob Prince at Forbes Field on the 45th anniversary of the first baseball broadcast on Aug. 5, 1966.

Broadcasting from Station WJZ

"Long George" Kelly (far left), who batted in the winning runs for the Giants in the 1921 World Series, is testing Station WJZ, from which play-by-play descriptions of the game were broadcast.

Forbes Field to broadcast the traditional rivalry between the Panthers and West Virginia. The microphone Arlin used was shaped like a round oatmeal box, fashioned of metal and lined with felt to filter out the noises from the field. Arlin sat in the stands with the inquisitive fans surrounding the radio apparatus. Led by All-Americans Tom Davies and Herb Stein, Pitt defeated the Mountaineers 21-14.

That Pitt-West Virginia broadcast beat the November 24, 1921 broadcast of the Texas-Texas A&M game in College Station on Thanksgiving Day. The events of the game were heard almost immediately in Austin via a wireless account sent by two Aggie cadets, W.A. Tolson and Harry Saunders, who transmitted a play-by-play over station 5XB in College Station to 5XU in Austin. Amateur wireless buffs elsewhere in Texas also picked up the broadcast, which was used by the *Austin American* as a supplementary story on the game, which ended in a 0-0 tie despite Texas being a huge favorite.

By the fall of 1921, Westinghouse had added two more stations. Joining KDKA were WJZ in Newark, New Jersey, and WBZ in Springfield, Massachusetts. Thousands of people were either buying crystal-set receivers or fashioning their own out of oatmeal boxes and wire. Poles were sprouting like slender young saplings from rooftops and backyards. Homemade aerials could pull in not only the Westinghouse stations but also the new WEAF in New York. Yet there were many who still thought radio was a passing fancy. Even the imaginative author H.G. Wells said "the whole broadcast industry will dry up."

After the Dempsey-Carpentier fight, the next benchmark broadcast was the all-New York 1921 World Series between the Yankees and the Giants. The three Westinghouse stations hooked up a direct line to the Polo Grounds. Renowned sportswriter Grantland Rice handled the play-by-play while WJZ announcer Tommy Cowan supplied half-inning bulletins on WJZ. Arlin did the same on KDKA. The Yankees won the first two games, but the Giants rallied to win the series five games to three. Among

the interviews that Rice conducted during the broadcasts were Giants first baseman George Kelly, recently appointed commissioner Kennesaw Mountain Landis, and heavyweight boxing champion Jack Dempsey.

Like Arlin in Pittsburgh, Tommy Cowan was WJZ's pioneer announcer. The station was in a converted cloakroom in the Westinghouse factory in Newark. Cowan had joined the Thomas Edison Laboratory in West Orange, New Jersey, and eventually gravitated into radio. "Everybody thought the whole thing was going to blow up," Cowan said in an August 1969 interview, just a few months before his death at age 85. "I lived at the station, coming in early and not leaving until 11:30 at night since Mr. Edison would think nothing of starting an experiment at half past eight in the evening, and we stayed until he was finished."

Cowan was responsible for introducing famous bandleader Vincent Lopez to radio. Lopez was playing at the Pennsylvania Grill in New York, and since Cowan forgot to ask Lopez about the program, he asked Lopez to introduce it. Extremely nervous, Lopez said, "Hello, everybody, Lopez speaking." It was the first appearance of a live dance band on radio. That greeting became synonymous with Vincent Lopez as he became one of the greats of early radio. Cowan, who also introduced Ed Wynn to radio, retired from WNYC in New York in 1961. During his long career, he was also proclaimed New York's official greeter, working with mayors such as James J. Walker and Fiorello LaGuardia.

The year 1922 saw radio and sports take some giant leaps forward. On June 26, J. Andrew White announced the welterweight championship fight between champion Jack Britton and challenger Benny Leonard at New York's Velodrome. More than 250,000 listeners within a radius of 800 miles tuned in the WJZ broadcast, which was the first event in sportscasting history that was not telephoned back to the originating station before it was sent out. At 94th Street and Broadway, two loudspeakers were extended from second-story windows, and people were packed underneath listening to the fight. At Times Square the crowd became so

Harold Arlin and Lowell Thomas in 1939. Arlin was the first to broadcast a major league baseball game on Aug. 5, 1921.

great that the manager of a radio shop had to lessen the volume because it could be heard at the Claridge Hotel, 250 yards away.

On July 27, 1922, White returned to Boyles's Thirty Acres to describe the Leonard-Lew Tendler lightweight title bout. One observer said it was the clincher. Radio in sports was here to stay. "In the future, no sporting event of major importance will be complete without it."

Grantland Rice was once again behind the microphone for the 1922 World Series between the Yankees and Giants, this time teamed with another sportswriter, W.O. "Bill" McGheehan. Radio-conducted "Player Boards" were set up in several larger cities, and the progress of the

game was marked on a giant chart. For years the public had been accustomed to the remarkable speed shown by the newspapers in providing mechanical and electric boards, but the radio boards would beat the newspaper boards by about half a minute. Near City Hall in New York, one street with radio boards showed the Giants scoring a run and a big cheer erupted. Thirty seconds later, on another street, came a similar roar as the newspaper board posted the same run. The immediacy of radio was undeniable.

Rice wrote afterwards in the *New York Tribune*, "It was just as if we had been doing this same thing for 20 years, showing again how quickly human nature adjusts itself to the ways of science and the sudden shocks of modern

Quin Ryan, of WGN in Chicago, 1924.

existence, where the impossible takes place every 15 or 20 minutes throughout the day." Wrote Glenn Scott in *Wireless Age* magazine: "We radio listeners lived the series as did they who were actually in the stands. And we did it in the comfort of our homes, or in our offices, leaning back in a chair, with our feet on the boss's desk."

Rice's voice was heard not only in homes and offices, but also by ships out at sea, by lighthouse keepers, the sick, the shut-ins, the farmers and the factory workers. "We heard the ovation given Jack Dempsey as he entered the stand," wrote Scott. "We heard the cheering for Christy Mathewson, who came to see and write about the game after his two-year successful battle against tuberculosis. Several times we even heard the crack of the bat on the nose of the ball—or was it just our imagination? We all but saw!"

Immediately following the great success with the World Series, WJZ broadcast the college football season beginning with Colgate at Princeton and culminating with the Army-Navy game in Philadelphia on November 25. Hockey made its radio debut when the legendary Foster Hewitt, who would broadcast NHL hockey for 50 years, announced the Toronto Parkdales against the Kitchener Seniors in March 1923. The first hockey broadcasts in the United States began on station WEEI in Boston in December 1926. Station WNAC in Boston broadcast the first college baseball game at Harvard in 1922. WNAC was also the first to air a golf tournament, on April 4, 1926, and the first wrestling match in September 1927. The Indianapolis 500 race in 1924 was broadcast by A.W. "Sen" Kaney on WDAP in Chicago, the forerunner of WGN, while J. Andrew White announced the first horse race from Belmont Park on WJZ on September 1, 1924.

🔘 Quin Ryan: CD 1: Track 13

In August 1924, Kaney soon gave way on the WGN sports scene to a young Northwestern University student actor, columnist, and broadcaster named Quin A. Ryan, who had been editing the *Chicago Tribune's* in-house organ. One of Ryan's first broadcasts was on October 18, 1924, when Illinois hosted Michigan as Illinois' new Memorial Stadium

Vernon Rickard (left) and Quin Ryan supplied the sound effects for the first Punch and Judy Show broadcast in 1925.

was dedicated before a packed house of 67,000. Red Grange scored four touchdowns in the first 12 minutes as the Illini won 39-14. Perched on the roof of the vast new stadium, Ryan revealed with delight that the Illini came on the field bare-legged (an innovation) and that Grange wore number 77, the same number as the Michigan fans' special train.

Ryan became the jack of all trades on WGN. On New Year's Day 1925, he sat in the Drake Hotel studio and broadcast by ticker tape the Tournament of Roses parade, plus the Rose Bowl itself won by Notre Dame over Stanford, 27-10, in the final game of the fabled "Four Horsemen" of Notre Dame and the legendary Ernie Nevers at Stanford. Ryan broadcast the first Kentucky Derby in 1925, and on Memorial Day of the same year, he broadcast his first Indianapolis 500, describing "the roar of the racing cars as they flash by the stands traveling 100 miles an hour."

The first coast-to-coast World Series broadcast was undertaken in 1925 with a network of two legs, or chains—the eastern leg and the western leg—and this time, Judge Landis picked the announcers. Ryan and a young tenor-turned-broadcaster named Graham McNamee were chosen. There were no sponsorships.

"At the Derby, WGN broadcast interviews, band concerts and every race including the Derby, without returning to the studio," said Ryan in recalling those early days. "At Indianapolis I did the same for seven hours, interviewing famous drivers such as Barney Oldfield, Gar Wood, Gaston Chevrolet and Eddie Rickenbacker. Microphones were placed in the pits, along the track and other places so that thousands of listeners said they were ducking their heads when the whizzing cars threatened to jump right out of their radios." Helping Ryan on the Derby and 500 broadcasts were two young comics named Freeman Gosden and Charles Correll, then called Sam 'n' Henry, who would later become Amos 'n' Andy in 1928.

Ryan's sports descriptions made a great impression on a youngster growing up in Iowa named Ronald Reagan. "Quin was the father of sports broadcasting," said Reagan, who began his storied career in movies and politics as a sportscaster. "It was Quin who got the idea that you could sit and describe a baseball game and make someone else see it. In just a few years Quin had created a profession."

Ryan's versatility saw him broadcast eight Republican and Democratic conventions, ten Kentucky Derbies and Indianapolis 500 races, World Series, sailboat races, daily broadcasts of the Cubs and White Sox games, and seventeen college football seasons. Amazingly adaptable, he also became a fixture doing children's programs, which he hosted for 19 years. He was Uncle Quin to a throng of youngsters who grew up listening to him broadcast the Sunday comics. In 1931, Ryan broadcast Knute Rockne's funeral in South Bend. Wrote the Rev. Charles E. Pettit of the Bloomington, Illinois, Methodist Church: "No more colorful, appropriate and beautiful English have I ever heard than from your announcer."

There wasn't anything Quin didn't do on WGN. He became WGN's general manager in 1930 and served for more than ten years. It was while in that post that he had to curtail his daily broadcasts of Cubs and White Sox games.

Radio Age magazine conducted the first radio popularity poll in 1924 with the "Solemn Old Judge" of Nashville, George Hay, number one. Second was WEAF announcer Graham McNamee, and in fourth place was Harold Arlin of KDKA in Pittsburgh.

Arlin was establishing quite a reputation at KDKA. In the British Isles, his name was a household word, and his voice was heard as far away as Australia. Housewives in Melbourne worried about his health if he chanced to cough during an announcement.

Radio always tried to go to the scene for authenticity's sake. For instance, when famed orator William Jennings Bryan made his radio debut on KDKA, Arlin introduced him from the pulpit of an empty church several miles from the station. Arlin's list of introductions read like a "Who's Who" of the times: Herbert Hoover, David Lloyd George, World War I Allied Commander Marshall Foch,

Lillian Gish, and Will Rogers, to name a few. "Will Rogers arrived at the studio, picked up a copy of the *Pittsburgh Sun* and commented for 20 minutes on the air about the problems of the country," remembered Arlin. "To this day I have never heard a more humorous demonstration of extemporaneous wit."

In late 1925, with his radio popularity at its height, Arlin abandoned his radio career almost as swiftly as it started. He was still working a regular job during the day at the Westinghouse plant, and he would broadcast on the radio station at night. When he heard about a job opening in the personnel department at the Westinghouse factory in Mansfield, Ohio, he took it.

Stunned by the move, newspaper headlines read, "One of the Best Known Voices in the World Will Become Silent." Another newspaper wrote, "Thousands of Radio Fans Will Regret Loss of Popular Friend."

Arlin was never bitten again by the radio bug. Instead he never missed a day in 43 years in the Westinghouse industrial relations department. He became a civic leader in Mansfield, was president of the school board for 16 years, and despite his protestations had a 12,000-seat high school football stadium, Arlin Field, named in his honor. A delight in his later years was to watch his grandson Steve Arlin pitch for the Padres and Indians in a big-league career that spanned six seasons in the early 1970s.

Harold occasionally returned to Pittsburgh to celebrate anniversaries on KDKA, sitting in on Pirate radio broadcasts with Bob Prince.

Arlin passed away on March 14, 1986, at the age of 90. He, like Florent Gibson, J. Andrew White, Tommy Cowan, Quin Ryan, and others were true sportscasting pioneers. Long ago forgotten, they helped usher in the golden age of radio sports.

Despite its success in building interest, and with it, bigger crowds at the gate, there was still concern about radio giving the public something for nothing. W.O. "Bill" McGheehan, who helped Grantland Rice broadcast the 1922 World Series, turned prophet in a 1925 article predicting that the not-yet-developed medium called "television" would threaten sports survival. "Dipping only casually into the future, one can see the time coming when thousands of 'radio cinemas' are dumped upon the market. Persons possessing these machines will be able to sit in their homes and watch a World Series without having to contribute to the gate receipts. It sounds very ominous for the promoters of professional sports."

Later, in the 1930s, there were objections to radio from several minor-league club owners, who opposed the infiltration of major-league broadcasts into their territories. In April 1936, Commissioner Landis ordered that no additional commitments, arrangements or authorizations for radio broadcasts of games be made by major or minor-league clubs, pending an investigation that the airing of games was seriously harming home attendance in certain parks. As a result, in 1937, stations were forced to pay the clubs for the privilege of broadcasting their games, but the airing of games nevertheless soared to new highs.

Bans were lifted in the American Association as well as the International and Texas Leagues, and sponsors' rates soared, with General Mills spending over one million dollars in 1937. Wheaties commercials were heard in every big-league city and most of the top minor-league towns. Competition came from the Socony gasoline company, Kellogg's Corn Flakes, General Foods, Texaco and the Atlantic Refining Company ("Come out and see the game. This is the broadcast for those who can't come"). In short, owners, depleted as they were by the effects of the Great Depression, expenditures and other discouragements, looked on radio as an unexplored new area of possible revenue.

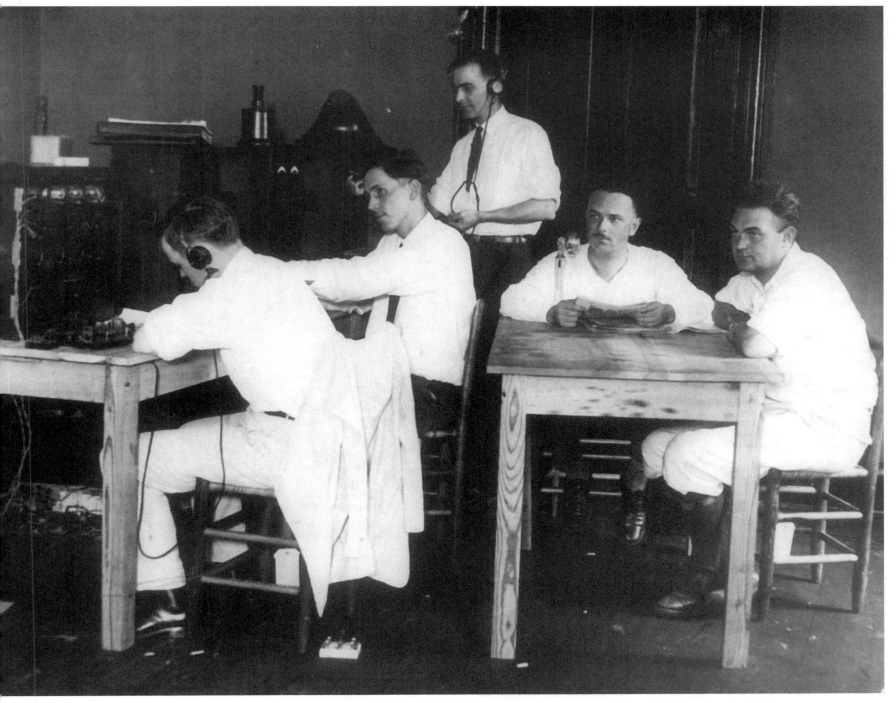

Quin Ryan (holding script), prepares to broadcast from Dayton, Tennessee in 1925. WGN broadcast day-to-day proceedings of the Scopes "Monkey Trial."

Ted Patterson portrait of Graham McNamee and the "Texaco Star Chief," Ed Wynn.

ON THE AIR

WITH RED SOX BASEBALL
FROM WHDH-RADIO—WHDH-TV

CURT GOWDY

NED MARTIN

ART GLEESON

SPECIAL RED SOX BASEBALL EDITION
For 1962 From
NEW ENGLAND'S BIG LEAGUE STATIONS!

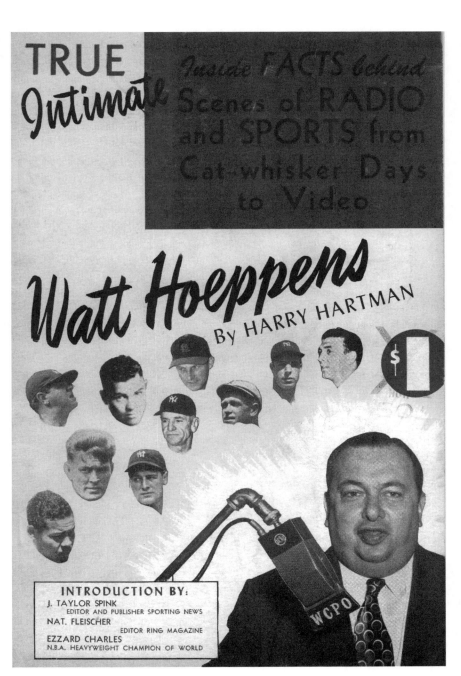

TRUE *Intimate* Inside FACTS behind Scenes of RADIO and SPORTS from Cat-whisker Days to Video

Watt Hoeppens
By HARRY HARTMAN

$1

INTRODUCTION BY:
J. TAYLOR SPINK
EDITOR AND PUBLISHER SPORTING NEWS
NAT. FLEISCHER
EDITOR RING MAGAZINE
EZZARD CHARLES
N.B.A. HEAVYWEIGHT CHAMPION OF WORLD

WCPO

THE BIG THREE

On the morning of May 10, 1942, the day after Graham McNamee died at the age of 53 of a strep infection, the brilliant rays of the California setting sun cast their glowing warmth over the gray Sierra Madre Mountains. But the sight would never be quite as glorious a spectacle as it was that late New Year's Day afternoon in 1927, when McNamee wandered away from the description of the Rose Bowl game to talk about the golden splendor of the sunset. It would always remain McNamee's sunset, so memorable was his description.

His breathless broadcasts brought delight to millions, whether they were of a heavyweight title fight or a political convention. McNamee's career spanned the first 20 years of radio, and he, more than anyone else, blazed the trail for those who followed. No president could be inaugurated or title fight staged without Graham McNamee being there.

Born in Washington D.C. in 1889, he grew up hoping to become a singer and headed for New York to study music seriously. One afternoon in 1923, McNamee, out of curiosity, wandered into the studios of WEAF on Broadway. Within an hour the young tenor's life was changed forever. Program director Sam Ross thought McNamee—with his great voice, knowledge, and diction—was a natural.

McNamee was far from a sports expert, yet it was in sports that he specialized, especially in the early years of his career. He made his sports debut on August 21, 1923 at the Polo Grounds when middleweight champion Johnny Wilson defended his title against Harry Greb. He visited the camps of both fighters to gather information. The night of the fight he had a bad case of the jitters, knowing boxing fans could be more critical than music lovers. He calmed down during the prelims and during the main event was totally immersed

in describing the fight and all the color around it.

"Through it all, I tried to keep my head clear and coolly analyze a bit," McNamee recalled years later. "The harder Greb was hit, the quicker came his smile, a strange recoil from blow to grin. It was hard not to pull for Greb. I had met his motherless daughter Dorothy in camp. She was only three but traveled with Harry after his wife died. When Wilson buckled Harry with a terrific blow to the head, I got so excited I couldn't speak. Although referee Jack O'Sullivan accused Greb of butting and other dirty tactics, Greb won 13 of the 15 rounds and left Wilson with a cut on his nose, a bleeding and torn mouth, puffed and raw lips, an almost closed left eye and a lump under his right eye. Greb was spitting blood but walked away with no facial marks."

McNamee's next big sports assignment came in October 1923, when the Yankees played the Giants in the World Series. A special wire was installed between WEAF and WGY. Before the fourth game in the new Yankee Stadium, writer Bill McGheehan, disgusted with the assignment, walked off the job during the fourth inning of the third game. McNamee had been assisting McGheehan but rarely speaking until then.

Unlike the Greb-Wilson fight with its non-stop action, McNamee found himself using his powers of description and imagination "to make the quieter times vivid and to avoid the old, hackneyed and boresome expressions." He explained, "You must make each of your listeners feel that he or she is with you in that press box, watching the movements of the game."

"The color and flags, the pop bottles thrown in the air. The straw hats demolished. Gloria Swanson arriving in her new ermine coat. John McGraw in his dugout, apparently motionless but giving signals all the time. The

Graham McNamee at the mike at the Waldorf Astoria on NBC's 15th anniversary in 1941.

pitcher beginning to waver and another preparing to come to the relief of his faltering comrade. The little things make a difference. Saying that 'Scott is knocking the mud from his cleats,' or 'Shawkey is tossing a few curves to loosen the kinks in his arm,' or 'The umpire is examining the ball to see if Meusel nicked it with his last single.' It looks absurd in print, but these little details add life to the game for the fellows who can't see it."

Concerning the temper tantrum thrown by McGheehan that prompted him to throw down his

microphone and walk away during the third game, respected baseball writer Fred Lieb of the *New York Evening Telegram* said McGheehan was an odd choice to be picked in the first place. "Bill was not a loquacious man, and he was quite moody. You could be with him for half an hour without him uttering a word." Lieb continued, "When he did say something it was usually in short sentences." Lieb actually was part of the 1923 broadcast, as McNamee asked him to do a 15-minute recap after game two. "I don't know how I found time to do it," said Lieb. "I was the official

Fred Lieb (right) and Rogers Hornsby in 1927 before the microphones.

Graham McNamee interviewing Babe Ruth on the sidelines in 1926.

scorer of the series, handled the press arrangements and wrote my story for the *New York Evening Telegram*."

McNamee was soon teamed with a young announcer named Phillips Carlin. Like McNamee, Carlin's knowledge of sports was limited. Even McNamee admitted he was an entertainer first and a broadcaster second. After McNamee's broadcast of the 1924 World Series in which Washington beat the Giants four games to three, this letter came from an irate Senators fan: "I have reference to the partiality of the announcer Graham McNamee in favor of the Giants. It was to such an extreme degree that it caused unfavorable comment from all over the country. It was headlines in the Washington press."

The issue of impartiality was discussed for the first time as listeners were becoming more particular and critical. Wrote a New York fan: "Why, the Washington players couldn't even brush the dust off their pants or pull down their caps without it being a 'beautiful play.'"

In 1925, McNamee sat in the rain describing the Pirates' 9-7 win over Walter Johnson and the Senators at soggy Forbes Field. Rain was pouring down his neck while he covered his microphone with his jacket. Noted writer Heywood Broun penned a stirring tribute to Graham after listening to the broadcast. "He made me feel the temperature and the tension. The wind hit him and was deflected off to me. McNamee allowed you to follow the ball on the wing. To listen was just as exciting as to see it. A thing may be a marvelous invention and still dull as ditch water. McNamee has been able to take a new medium of expression and through it transmit himself—to give out vividly a sense of movement and feeling. Of such is the kingdom of art."

But accuracy wasn't McNamee's forté. Before the first game of the 1926 World Series, McNamee asked Lieb to bring National League president John Heydler to the radio booth. "Graham made a flowery introduction of Heydler, calling him a man we all know, a former great pitcher who made his niche in banking, in Congress and as governor of Pennsylvania," said Lieb. "He then introduced him as John K. Tener, who had resigned the National League presidency in 1918, eight years before." One fan wrote after the 1925 World Series: "You failed in 1924, but, my God, you get worse as you get older! Stick to music and weather reports, but let the Chicago man [Quin Ryan] handle the large

athletic events for the good of us all."

Eventually Baseball Commissioner Kenesaw Mountain Landis saw fit to remove McNamee from the Series broadcasts.

McNamee followed no rules. The game and the color around it were the thing, and his "wow" and "whees" and exclamations of wonder and amazement punctuated his running descriptions. He was always conscious of the fact he was "Mr. Radio" to millions of people, and he demanded and expected preferential treatment.

After the NBC network was formed in November 1926, McNamee broadcast the first coast-to-coast hookup of the Rose Bowl on New Year's Day, 1927. Four thousand miles of wire had to be strung to enable the nation to listen to Alabama and Stanford play to a 7-7 tie. That Rose Bowl was the game where McNamee colorfully described the sunset behind the mountains into which Pasadena was tucked.

At the 1927 World Series between the Yankees and the Pirates, writer Ring Lardner sat in an adjoining seat to the NBC radio booth where Graham was broadcasting. "It was like attending a doubleheader," wrote Lardner in his column the following day. "You saw one game and heard another."

At the Gene Tunney-Tom Heeney fight at Yankee Stadium on July 23, 1928, Tunney, in his last fight, won by knocking out the Australian eight seconds before the end of the eleventh round. Punches were flying from Tunney's fists so fast that McNamee was several wallops behind in his description. When the fight was stopped, Graham paid no attention, because he had to read a live tire commercial that lasted 60 seconds. He waited for the twelfth round to begin and didn't realize the fight was over. The radio audience was left totally in the dark as McNamee packed up and left the arena, content to let the fans read the result in the morning newspapers.

As radio became more sophisticated and audiences more demanding, McNamee's popularity began to fade. To Graham, every fighter was a Dempsey, every batter a Babe Ruth, every fight the battle of the century. By the late 1930s, he was doing mostly newsreel voiceovers. His enthusiasm for sports waned as he got older. He said goodbye to the radio listeners for the last time on April 14, 1942 as the

Ted Husing, who first started broadcasting with WJZ in New York.

announcer on *Elsa Maxwell's Party Line*: "This is Graham McNamee, saying 'Goodnight all, and goodbye.'" He entered the hospital the next day. Less than a month later he was dead.

Over a span of 19 years, Graham McNamee's voice was heard by more people than any other man alive. His dream was to retire to California so that he could witness that glorious sunset he described at the Rose Bowl. Unfortunately he never got that chance.

The Roaring Twenties were a golden decade in literature, movies, music, and, perhaps more than anything, sports. Every sport had its legendary names. Jack Dempsey and Tex Rickard's million-dollar gates ruled boxing, Walter Hagen and Bobby Jones dominated golf, Bill Tilden and Helen Wills were king and queen of tennis, Red Grange was running roughshod over the gridirons of the Midwest in football, and Knute Rockne was coaching Notre Dame to greatness. In baseball, Babe Ruth had personally saved the sport from near ruination over the 1919 Black Sox scandal. Radio, of course, was helping to make these great athletes larger than life.

 **Ted Husing**: CD 1: Track 14

At about the time Graham McNamee was making his mark as one of the most versatile announcers on the air, a young 23-year-old roustabout began broadcasting on WJZ. His name was Ted Husing, and he, more than anybody, elevated the job of sports broadcasting to a profession. Husing combined a great voice with knowledge of his subject into vivid and accurate descriptions that set the standards for all the sports announcers that followed. "If there had been more announcers like Ted Husing, they probably never would have thought of television," wrote Leon Rasmussen of the *New York Morning Telegraph* in 1957. "The vivid, animated, accurate word pictures he was able to draw with his golden-toned voice have never been matched, hardly approached, in the history of sports reporting on radio or television."

Husing was the prototype of the perfect

Ted Husing and Les Quailey in 1933, the day before the Ohio State-Michigan game in Ann Arbor.

sportscaster. He was blessed with a great voice but never depended upon it alone. He was prepared and knew his subject and never groped for words; he had the right one for every occasion—not dull, stereotyped clichés, but proud, descriptive words made ever more graphic by action-packed verbs that brought the game rocketing right into your room.

Husing was born on November 27, 1901, in Deming, New Mexico. The family moved east as Husing's father became a steward at a Columbia University club. Young Ted served as mascot of the Columbia University football, baseball, basketball and soccer teams. These years served as the foundation of his sports knowledge. At Commerce High School, he played baseball and football and met a boy named Les Quailey, who later became the chief assistant on his broadcasts.

Husing remained in high school for just a couple of years before quitting. He bummed around the country working in street carnivals, helping in Midwestern wheat fields, and punching cows. Upon his return to New York, he was fired from several jobs before answering an ad in the *New York Times* for a radio announcer at station WJZ. He responded by giving himself a college degree and informing the station of his love of opera and symphonic music, of which he knew nothing. As it turned out, he competed with 610 applicants over 14 days of tests to get the job. "If they didn't actually ask to see the sheepskin, I felt I might possibly get away with the cultural part of it. Maybe I had grown up on the sidewalks of New York, but I wasn't exactly a 'dese-dose' guy," wrote Husing in his 1935 book, *Ten Years Before the Mike*. The group of more than 600 was whittled to six, and it was the musical knowledge that was knocking off most of them. Music was the principal focus of radio, but extemporaneous speaking was also vital, and Husing was a master of the ad-lib.

Husing came clean with the assistant studio manager, who had taken a liking to him and who taught him enough music to get him through. Next came extemporizing, and Husing talked aviation and a bad air crash that had

happened out west. He talked for more than 30 minutes and got the job, which paid $45 a week. The date was September 13, 1924.

"Ted was a master ad-libber," remembered his longtime partner Jimmy Dolan, who spent several decades as an executive with CBS. "He studied the English language and liked big words. He was always in control of his voice. He could bring you to the edge of your seat without screaming. He had a sense of pacing and an ability to transfer what he saw very accurately. He loved the language, the sound of it and the flow of it."

Husing's first sports assignment was the Penn-Cornell football game at the new Franklin Field in Philadelphia in 1925. He was supposed to observe J. Andrew White broadcast the game, but White didn't show up, and Husing went on cold to a hookup that included Boston, Washington and Pittsburgh. "I described the weather and set the scene, but I couldn't talk about the teams, because I didn't know anything about them," said Husing afterwards. White suddenly showed up, unprepared, and relied on Husing's scribbled notes for much of his information. White appreciated the help and told Husing he would let him be their football announcer in 1926.

The following year, though, Husing took a radio job in Boston where he broadcast the home games of the Boston Braves. He returned to New York in the fall as a freelancer, broadcasting 16 football games on WHN, including the entire Columbia schedule.

During that time, J. Andrew White became president of the fledgling Columbia Broadcasting System and offered Husing the job of assistant to the president. Husing began his CBS work on Christmas Day, 1927, with WOR as the flagship station. In 1928, he shared the microphone duties for the Yankees-Cardinals World Series as well as the U.S. Open tennis championships at Forest Hills. Just before 1928 ended, a wealthy young businessman named William S. Paley purchased the network and helped launch CBS and Husing into a new era.

Although admittedly Husing didn't know a horse from a Holstein, Paley sent him out to broadcast the muddy 1929 Kentucky Derby—won, as Husing described, by an unknown horse named Clyde Van Dusen. On rival NBC, the announcer at the finish line named Blue Larkspur, the favorite, as the winner.

During the race, Paley hosted a party and had two loudspeakers blaring both broadcasts. He had been bragging about the prowess of his young broadcaster, saying that even though Husing hadn't seen a race in his life, he'd still outdo the experts at NBC. Paley was right. Down the stretch Husing screamed, "Larkspur seems to be tiring. They're bunching up. A horse on the outside is closing the gap— it's—it's—it's Clyde Van Dusen! They're neck and neck, thundering down at us through the mud. What a finish! Van Dusen is out ahead by a length now as they pass here. Blue Larkspur is dropping back and it's over, Van Dusen wins the Derby!" At the same moment over NBC came the words, "Blue Larkspur wins!" The shouts of laughter at the Paley party drowned out the correction by NBC, and it wasn't until later that Paley's faith in his young announcer was indeed justified.

Although he excelled in all sports, Husing was unmatched in broadcasting tennis, track and golf. "I'd like to hear an announcer today attempt on radio to broadcast a doubles tennis match," recalled Husing's assistant Quailey. "That would really be something." In 1930, Husing used the first portable transmitting apparatus ever, jogging beside a runner at the Penn Relays. He used it again at the 1930 National Amateur as he followed Bobby Jones around the course. One of Husing's great thrills was describing Jones winning the U.S. Open that year, when he took all four major championships. Leading McDonald Smith by a stroke on the 18th hole, Jones, confronting a 40-foot putt, gave it a little tap. Husing described how the ball started down hill, gathered speed, caught the side of a slope and rolled to the right, then up another slope and down again before reaching level ground,

losing momentum, and then trickling straight and true for the center of the hole, dropping in.

Husing was easily the top sportscaster in the business throughout the 1930s. "Whenever I broadcast," he told a reviewer, "I always imagine myself in the listener's shoes, trying to imagine what would interest me most if I were sitting at home listening." As another reviewer once said of him: "Mind, eye, ear and tongue work as one—and the nose smells news."

After 19 years at CBS, during which time he became radio's highest paid announcer, the always unpredictable Husing surprised everybody by quitting to become a disc jockey for WMGM for a salary in the $250,000 range. Husing's *Bandstand* was so popular that the Brooklyn Dodgers, heard on the same station, were forced to play their afternoon games earlier because his show began at 5 p.m. It made no matter if the game was tied in the 11th inning. Husing took precedence.

Rather than adapt to television and its reduced need for chatter, Husing broadcast a televised event as if he was on radio. When he did an early TV fight, a writer commented that he was talking too much. This upset him, and on the next fight broadcast he hardly talked at all. "Ted never did reach a happy medium with television, and Ted never compromised with anybody or anything," Quailey said.

In the early 1950s, a noticeable limp and pain in his spine forced Husing to seek medical attention. After months of examinations and tests he was diagnosed with a brain tumor. Several surgeries, beginning in 1954, cost him his sight and, for a while, his speech. He was only 55 when his condition was declared virtually hopeless.

At the 10th annual Sports Broadcasters Association banquet in 1956, Husing, a man of great pride, stood at the microphone and tearfully said, "Tonight, one does not need eyes. For one has eyes in his heart." He tried an unsuccessful comeback with CBS in 1957, when his health improved, but in February 1958, he moved to his mother's modest

Bill Munday (right) broadcasting with Ernie Harwell on the left and station manager Sam Kane looking on.

Pasadena, California cottage. Near the end he was paralyzed as well as sightless. Husing died on August 10, 1962, at the age of 60.

"A great deal was said about the qualities that made him great," wrote famed columnist Red Smith. "About his voice, his gift of gab, and about how he could dramatize the event he was covering. Everything they said was true, but nobody came out with the real reason he has never been touched—his painstaking quest for accuracy that made him the most knowledgeable reporter on the air. Nobody ever worked harder at learning the game he was broadcasting."

Although McNamee and Husing were bigger names on the national radio scene, Bill Munday was certainly the most colorful and unique member of the trio known in the early days of radio as "The Big Three." With an unmistakable southern drawl and a football vocabulary which spoke of "crapshooter's formations and Beulah Land," Munday became the most famous football announcer in the South. He called the last 12 inches between the ball and the goal line "the most valuable piece of Georgia real estate between Rabun Gap and Tybee Light." Off the microphone, Munday led a life of heartbreak that was brought on by alcoholism and his lifelong battle to overcome it.

An early compliment was paid Munday when *New York Daily News* writer Paul Gallico wrote on July 29, 1929: "Suddenly from the loudspeaker comes a fresh new voice, a voice that for all its southern cadences and rhythmics is letting fly a bristling, rapid fire of description, couched in a new and gay phraseology, teeming with good humor and enthusiasm, and demonstrating without ostentation how sports on radio should be spoken." Veteran major-league broadcaster Ernie Harwell worked with Munday in Atlanta

and felt that many announcers, including himself, copied Munday's style without knowing it.

"I know I have and I've always felt that Red Barber did too. It was a down-to-earth, southern homespun type of delivery with expressions that come from the kitchen table and the back yard," Harwell said.

Munday's fame, thanks to alcoholism, was fleeting. He ended up doing some public-address announcing for his beloved Georgia football team before suffering a heart attack in 1964. "I am a Bulldog born, a Bulldog bred, and when I die I'll be a Bulldog dead," he said near the end. He died on February 26, 1965.

Wrote Atlanta columnist John Martin the following day: "The old Bulldog slid through the ashes and dust into the home plate he immortalized as Beulah Land. He had done more for 'Beulah Land' than both the Bible and Bunyan. It was the end of the career of a southpaw hopeful who couldn't pitch himself into the majors, but who talked himself into the promised land of 'milk and honey' with a twang to please the hungry ear of the nation's 'loudspeaker ensemble.' He led two lives at opposite ends of the world. From obscurity he rocketed into the stratosphere, then tobogganed on a cork to the hinges of hell. His recovery outweighed all his fumbles. He had no enemies except John Barleycorn, the 100-proof slugger who knocked Munday out of his regular turn as an ace in the Big Three. Graham McNamee and Ted Husing were the other starters of this immortal triumvirate, but of the three, the old Georgia southpaw had more stuff. Maybe not as fast and sharp, but a better mixture, until Boss Barleycorn took him back and below the minors. So this fall when his cherished Bulldogs kick off, Bill won't be there to say 'he was brought to mother earth from whence he sprang.' Instead, he'll be a saintly spectator, watching silently from the 50-yard line, and his spirit and heart will be in Sanford Field. He'll be hoping it's a good day, ladies and gentlemen.'"

The 1948 All-Star game preview on the Mutual network. From left, Yankee great Joe Dimaggio, Dan Topping, France Laux. Seated, Del Webb, Mel Allen, Mutual sports director Paul Jonas, baseball commissioner Happy Chandler and announcer Bob Ingham.

Two shots of the 1936 World Series broadcasters for CBS. France Laux and Boake Carter were behind the microphones with engineer Paul White with headphones on the front row.

Top: *Gene Kelly (far left), Claude Haring (second from left), and Byrum Saam (second from right), the Phillies broadcasters, pose at the Bayuk Cigar Factory in 1958. The factory sponsored the broadcasts.*

Top: *The 1936 World Series broadcasters for CBS, engineer Paul White (left), Boake Carter (center) and France Laux (right).*

Bottom: *1965 shot of several announcers and players-turned-announcers. Back row: Mel Parnell, Bob Delaney, unknown man, Curt Gowdy and Don Hoak. Kneeling: Byrum Saam, Ned Martin, Bob Prince, Jim Woods and Bill Campbell.*

Bottom: *Red Barber and Mel Allen (middle back row) stand side by side while a young Vin Scully, Connie Desmond and Al Helfer man the front row, circa 1951.*

TAKE ME OUT TO THE BALLGAME

"When I get lonesome and homesick, the most wonderful remedy is to pick up the baseball game on short-wave and to know that I am listening to the same game, the same announcers, the same words that my dad is hearing back home."

—A G.I. letter to Armed Forces Radio, World War II

In this age of cable, computers and billion-dollar network contracts, where every major-league game is broadcast on radio and practically every game is televised, only a small portion of the populace can hearken back to another time when just listening to a big-league game on radio as it was actually being played provided an exhilarating thrill for young and old fans alike.

From the feeble beginnings on KDKA and the early World Series broadcasts on WEAF, it didn't take long for radio stations to realize the impact that broadcasting baseball would have on listenership.

Several big-league owners, however, were not as farsighted as the radio pioneers. Barney Dreyfuss in Pittsburgh and the owners of the three New York teams barred live broadcasts from their parks for years. It wasn't until Larry MacPhail brought Red Barber to Brooklyn in 1939 that the New York ban was lifted.

Chicago, on the other hand, was one of the pacesetters in the airing of games. In 1924, the *Chicago Daily News* radio station, WMAQ, began regular broadcasts of the Chicago Cubs. A young *Daily News* rewrite man, Hal Totten, quickly volunteered to be the announcer, thinking it an excellent way to view the games for free. Cubs owner William Wrigley, Jr. desired a former player to handle the broadcasts and called on former Cub Solly Hoffman. Hoffman lasted just one day, however, completely overwhelmed by the job. Totten was on the air the following day with his famous "G'bye now" signoff, remaining for 19 years through the 1943 season.

In the early years, the American League had a rule prohibiting the broadcasting of games, but White Sox owner Charles Comiskey told league officials he was going to air Sox games whether they liked it or not. Comiskey wielded some clout, and as soon as the ban was lifted, Totten began doing both the Cubs and the White Sox home games.

Hal Totten was born in Newark, New Jersey in 1901, and raised in Ithaca, New York before the family moved to Chicago in 1912. While attending Northwestern University, he took a part-time job at the *Daily News* and was soon broadcasting baseball, football, boxing and other events. He had totaled more than 25,000 events by the time he retired. One of his remembered assignments was broadcasting the second Dempsey-Tunney fight at Soldier Field in 1927.

"I'll never forget it," he recalled, "because my son John was born in the morning, I broadcast a doubleheader in the afternoon, and covered the fight that night."

After World War II, Totten moved to Keolua, Iowa, where he purchased a radio station. In 1950 he returned as a substitute announcer on Mutual's *Game of the Day* before leaving broadcasting to become president of the Three-I League in 1951 and president of the Southern Association in 1960.

Chicago quickly became the mecca of baseball broadcasting as five other stations airing the same games at the same time joined Totten within a period of five years. There were Quin Ryan and Bob Elson on WGN, Pat Flanagan on WBBM, Johnny O'Hara (and later Russ Hodges) over at WJJD, Jimmy Dudley and Jack Drees on WIND, and baseball immortal Tris Speaker on WENR. One station even hired the unlikely trio of Charlie Grimm, Lew Fonseca and Joe E. Brown to broadcast the action. It was possible for a youngster leaving school to walk home and never miss a play of the game because every single radio along the way had the ballgame tuned in.

The following section highlights some of the "superstars" of early broadcasting.

Above: *Hal Totten, announcer of all the Cubs and Sox games, is seen with his operator in 1925.*

Left: *Pioneer Chicago baseball broadcaster Hal Totten in 1926.*

CHICAGO BROADCASTERS

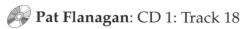 **Pat Flanagan**: CD 1: Track 18

Charles Carroll "Pat" Flanagan began broadcasting baseball in 1929 on WBBM and, like Hal Totten, continued through the 1943 season. Primarily a Cubs fan, Flanagan was one of the first to recreate road games off of a Western Union ticker, a task so nerve-wracking that it drove many broadcasters to drink.

Flanagan handled it with aplomb, however. It was said that his power of visualizing the tenseness of the action from a piece of paper bordered on "supernatural insight." Such was his prowess that many fans thought he was sitting in the stands broadcasting live, with one fan even calling the station to settle a bet as to where he was broadcasting the game.

Sponsored by Wheaties, he once asked listeners to drop him a line and enclose a Wheaties box top. The announcement drew 2,550 box tops from 211 counties in eight states.

Born in Clinton, Iowa in 1893, Flanagan graduated from Grinnell College, was a Silver Star winner in World War I and a faculty member of the Palmer School of Chiropractics in Davenport, Iowa, before getting his break in radio.

His first job on WOC, the Palmer radio station, was to sing songs, conduct exercises and teach philosophy. From there he joined WBBM, where his initial duties were heading the farm division and writing musical productions. Within a year he was doing baseball, and he worked several World Series and All-Star games on CBS.

"Pat was a Cubs fan first, last, and always," said his widow Hazel in 1967.

Pat Flanagan passed away in 1963 at the age of 70.

France Laux and Pat Flanagan in 1934.

Pat Flanagan behind the mike in 1932.

Pat Flanagan interviews Woody English of the Cubs before a 1929 World Series game.

Flanagan's counterpart with the White Sox was WJJD's Johnny O'Hara, who was just as partisan for the South Siders as Flanagan was for the Cubs. When the Cubs and White Sox tangled in their annual city series, the Flanagan-O'Hara rivalry was almost as heated as the play on the field. If O'Hara called a Cub runner out by a city block, Flanagan said the White Sox runner was out by a mile. Ironically, they were teamed by CBS to broadcast the first All-Star game in Chicago on July 6, 1933. Hal Totten announced the game on NBC.

O'Hara was a member of the Merchant Marine for seven years as a wireless operator before broadcasting Chicago baseball on WCFL in 1927. A few years later he joined WJJD. O'Hara departed for St. Louis in 1936.

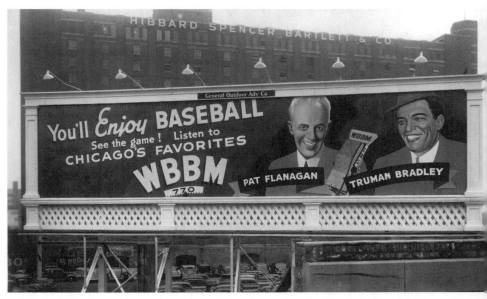

A Chicago billboard advertises WBBM and Pat Flanagan.

 **Bob Elson**: CD 1: Tracks 9-12

Bob Elson was the foundation of the Chicago baseball broadcasting fraternity. When he departed for Oakland in 1971, it sent shockwaves through the Windy City and ended a 40-year, 8,000-game span of announcing Cubs and White Sox games. Elson spent the last 25 of those seasons exclusively with the White Sox. One of Elson's proteges, Milo Hamilton, was still going strong in Houston in 2002.

Elson, nicknamed "The Commander," began his broadcasting career in 1928 almost as a gag. As a youngster growing up in Chicago, Elson sang in the famed Paulist Chorister Choir that toured in the United States and abroad. After transferring from Loyola of Chicago to Northwestern, he studied medicine. His love for baseball and reading box scores often took precedent over homework, however.

Between his sophomore and junior years of college, Elson took a trip to St. Louis and stayed at the Chase Hotel, which also was the headquarters of KWK radio. "The station was on the top floor. I had never seen how broadcasts were made, so I decided on a lark to take the elevator up to see what was going on," Elson said near the end of his career. "As things turned out it was the most important ride of my life."

Johnny O'Hara (right) with France Laux. The two broadcasters donned uniforms for the annual press-radio game in 1937.

Top: *Bob Elson with Lou Novikoff in 1941.*
Bottom: *Legendary Chicago broadcaster Bob Elson.*

When Elson entered the station, he discovered an announcers' contest was about to take place and that between 30 and 40 aspirants were crowded in the lobby. "Each man was escorted to a glass enclosed booth and given a script to read. Even though I had no experience, I decided to go along with the gag. I read some announcements and upon exiting was told I would be called if I were one of the three finalists. I now realized I was in a competition."

The next day Elson got a call from the station and was informed he was one of the three finalists. A panel of important St. Louis dignitaries, including the mayor and the Catholic Cardinal, eliminated one of the three, leaving Elson and another man vying for the job. The winner would be determined on an evening broadcast in which the public would listen to both candidates and vote for its favorite. "I got a call the next day saying I'd won," remembered Elson. "Before I even made up my mind on whether to accept the job, I got a call from the manager of WGN who had heard about the contest and offered me a job in Chicago. Since Chicago was my hometown, I took the offer immediately and announced my first WGN program on March 11, 1928. There went the career in medicine."

After a few months on the job, not happy with his early-morning job of introducing organ music, Elson told his boss he wanted to announce sporting events, then the domain of Quin Ryan. "A few days later Quin caught a bad cold, and I was told to stand by at Wrigley Field in case he had problems," recalled Elson. "He let me do a few innings, and with his cold worsening, I did the entire game the following day." The sponsors liked Bob more than Quin, who was really a football fan and was so spread out with his duties that he couldn't do baseball justice. By 1931 Elson was doing the entire home schedules of the White Sox and Cubs. "For well over a decade I worked all of the games myself," he said. "Doubleheaders, the show before the game, the show between games, postgame, 48 commercials and the play-by-play."

Elson considered baseball commissioner Landis one of his best friends and biggest boosters, and beginning in 1929, the commissioner appointed Elson to broadcast every World Series and All-Star game, an association that lasted until World War II. His favorite All-Star game was the 1941 classic in Detroit, when Ted Williams hit a dramatic three-run homer off Claude Passeau with two outs in the 9th that lifted the American League to a 7-5 win.

"The ball was hit so hard I thought it was going to land in my hotel suite," said Elson.

His most memorable Series was in 1934 when Tigers fans bombarded Ducky Medwick of the Cardinals with fruit, vegetables and assorted garbage for his hard slide into Marv Owen at third base the inning before. "I gave it to them on the air, tomato by tomato, pie by pie, without missing a lemon, banana or cabbage. I was in fine voice, and if the produce throwers could keep up the tempo, I knew I could," Elson said.

Medwick had to come off the field for order to be restored. The Cardinals won that seventh and deciding game with the Dean brothers, Dizzy and Daffy, winning all four games.

Elson was the first to do player interviews before games from the field, which he enjoyed as much as the game broadcasts. "Judge Landis gave me permission to run a mike down to the field. At first the players were nervous and hesitant. They gave stammering replies to stereotyped questions. That soon gave way to snappy, intelligent comments." Interviewing was Elson's forte, and in the 1950s he began doing an interview show from the famed Pump Room in Chicago. For five years he interviewed famous people on the Twentieth Century Limited passenger train.

In 1942, Elson entered the navy, and his protégé, Jack Brickhouse, replaced him. Elson became the first serviceman to announce a World Series in uniform when Landis asked him to do the 1943 series. Upon his discharge in 1946, he found a new climate in radio.

"No longer were there five stations doing the same

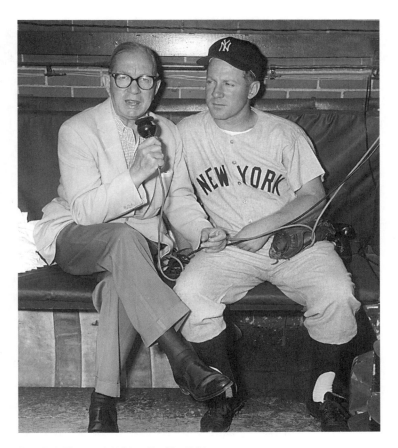

Top: *Bob Elson with Whitey Ford in 1961.*
Bottom: *Bob Elson with Casey Stengel in 1964. They were friends for forty years.*

Bob Elson reports on the Jim Londos/Strangler Lewis wrestling championship in the 1930s.

game, and no longer could one broadcaster divide his allegiance between two clubs. Since WGN wasn't doing the games in '46, I joined WJJD and cast my lot with the White Sox," Elson said.

The White Sox played in their last World Series in 1959, but Elson wasn't picked for the Series broadcast team. "Commissioner Ford Frick brought in Philadelphia's Byrum Saam to announce the Series, even though he had no association to the White Sox or the Dodgers. I had been with a losing ball club for almost 15 years, and here when the moment of glory arrived, I was denied the right to represent my team." It was a cruel snub, and the commissioner's office and the network were bombarded with mail protesting Elson's exclusion.

One Chicago writer, in talking about the Old Commander's longevity, said, "He's been in radio since the Kingfish of Amos 'n'Andy was a minnow and since Sox great Luke Appling was a little-leaguer." After winding up his White Sox career in 1970 with partner Red Rush on WMAQ, Elson spent a few seasons broadcasting Charlie Finley's Oakland Athletics before calling it quits. Elson died on March 13, 1981, at the age of 76.

When it came to partisanship, nobody topped Bert ("I don't care who wins as long as it's the Cubs") Wilson. "There is no such animal as a neutral Cub fan," he used to say. "If you like the Cubs, I make sense. If you don't, you won't tune in anyway."

Wilson's unabashed favoritism was even evident in his descriptions. He would never say the Giants were ahead by a run, but instead would say the Cubs were only a run behind. And he revived waning spirits with his motto, "It's never too late to start a rally." Broadcasting baseball literally killed Wilson. He became so excited towards the end of the 1952 season that he had to take two weeks off due to high blood pressure. He died in 1955 at the age of 44.

Jack Quinlan was in the prime of his life as the voice of the Chicago Cubs when he was killed in a car crash in March 1965, near the Cubs' spring training base in Mesa, Arizona. He was only 38 years old. "Jack Quinlan and WGN formed an unforgettable parlay," wrote WGN sports editor Jack Rosenberg after the announcer's sudden death. "Quinlan had the big sound, the sound which has brought the station greatness. His voice possessed the firmness of a hearty handshake. The resonance of a finely tuned harp, the clarity of a starry night. The quality of a prayer."

 Vince Lloyd: CD 2: Tracks 38-40

Vince Lloyd had a tough act to follow when he replaced Quinlan on Cubs broadcasts. He felt Quinlan was the best baseball announcer in the country. Interviewing President Kennedy on opening day in 1961 provided Lloyd with one of his greatest moments in broadcasting.

"I hosted a TV program called *Leadoff Man*, an interview usually with a player or coach," recalled Lloyd many years later. "The Sox had won the pennant in 1959, and we thought it would be a great way to start the season by interviewing the newly elected president. As it turned

Bert Wilson, voice of the Cubs, in the early 1950s.

Jack Quinlan, voice of the Cubs, in 1964.

out, I talked with him about 14 minutes. I was reluctant to ask him too many things about baseball because I wasn't sure how much he knew about the game. But he fielded every question dexterously, as did Vice President Johnson." Lloyd was a Peoria, Illinois protégé of Jack Brickhouse, as was Quinlan, and he teamed with Lou Boudreau to broadcast Cubs games for more than 15 years.

Certainly one of the tallest sportscasters in history, in the era before ex-athletes began manning the booths, was Jack Drees. A Chicago native who played basketball at Iowa, the lanky six-foot, six-inch Drees launched his broadcasting career at Iowa when he chose radio as a major. After graduating in 1938, Drees, surprisingly, was hired by WJJD to assist regular announcer John Harrington.

"The station was cutting corners after spending a lot of money to do live broadcasts from spring training on Catalina Island. Harrington needed a partner, and since they couldn't afford to hire anybody good, they hired me," explained Drees. He was paid $35 a week, a considerable wage in 1938.

The Cubs won the National League pennant in 1938, and Drees remembered broadcasting the game in which Gabby Hartnett homered in the gloamin' off Pittsburgh's Mace Brown to help clinch the flag.

"Darkness was emerging fast, and the Cubs pitching staff was exhausted to the point that if the Cubs didn't win the game they might not recover in time to win the pennant. The pandemonium in the park and in the broadcast booth was a memory I'll never forget," remembered Drees fondly.

Drees was soon doing Chicago Bears and Cardinals games, and when station WJJD and sister station WIND grew tired of fighting for one-fifth of the baseball audience, he began his career as a horse race caller, even though he had never been to a track before. Soon he was broadcasting seven races a day, six days a week, becoming one of the few sportscasters able to call a race capably.

"It is without question the most challenging undertaking that confronts a sports announcer," Drees emphasized. "For that two minutes of work, I flatter my ego by saying that you can have the greatest production in the world, but if the race isn't called well, you've had no show at all."

After 35 months of naval duty, 33 of them at sea, during World War II, Jack headed west to call races and serve as the PR director of the Los Angeles Dons in the All-America Football Conference. After the league folded following the 1949 season, he returned to the racetracks of Chicago before plunging into the new medium of television. His first assignment was with Russ Hodges on the Pabst Wednesday Night Fights, a position he held for 10 years. Drees returned to baseball in 1968 to televise White Sox games on WFLD for five seasons before Harry Caray took over on WSNS in 1973.

"When WFLD offered me the White Sox TV job, I called Lindsey Nelson to get his input, since he had joined the Mets full-time in 1962. Lindsey just said, 'Run, don't walk. It's the greatest. It's the best thing I ever did, and I know it'll be the best thing you ever did' Lindsey told me. And," added Drees, "it was."

Jack Drees in 1942.

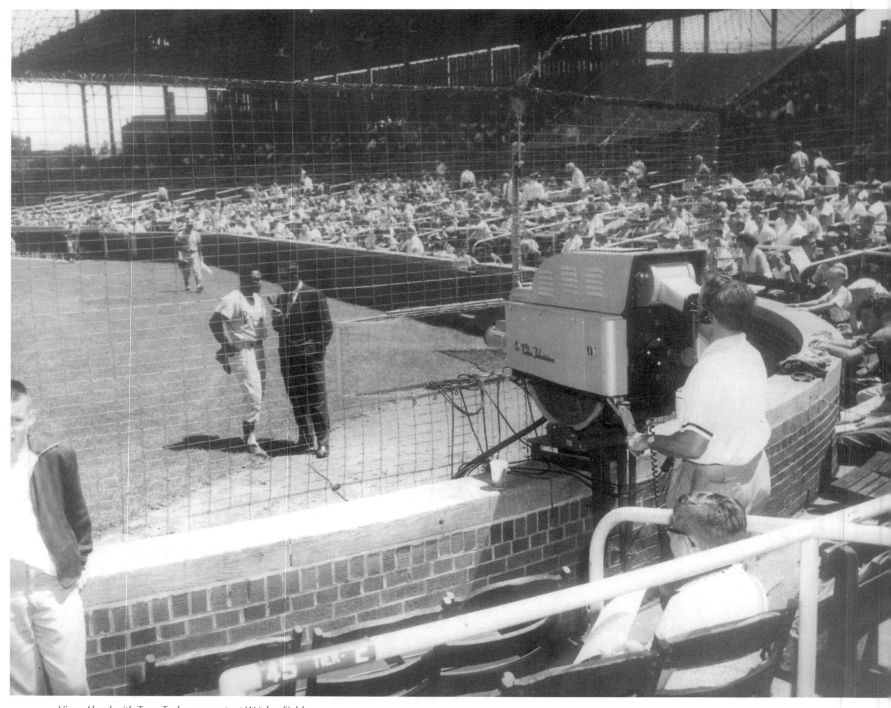

Vince Lloyd with Tony Taylor as guest, at Wrigley Field.

Cincinnati Broadcasters

Following in Chicago's pacesetting shoes, other cities began airing major-league baseball. Powell Crosley, Jr., who would one day own the Cincinnati Reds after making his fortune in the radio business, announced the first game in Cincinnati Reds history. Perched on the roof of the park that would one day bear his name, he announced the opening game of the 1927 season on his own station, WLW. Seven years later he purchased the Cincinnati ball club.

The first announcer to broadcast Cincinnati baseball on a regular basis was Bob Burdette on WLW. Burdette stationed himself in a shed on the grandstand roof of Redland Field. "The year was 1929," remembered the late historian of the Baseball Hall of Fame, Lee Allen. "The reason I know is that I was 14 years old in 1929 and remembered walking into Burdette's booth by accident just as he was running down the starting lineups. He announced that Leo Dixon, who batted only .167 in 14 games all season, was catching for the Reds. This so astonished me I blurted out 'Dixon!' at the top of my lungs, which went over the airways, drawing scowls from both Burdette and his engineer."

Although Red Barber was perhaps the best known and Waite Hoyt the most popular of all the Reds announcers over the years, certainly the most colorful was the loquacious Harry Hartman. It was in 1930 that Hartman—who stood only five feet, six inches tall but weighed close to 300 pounds and was employed by the *Cincinnati Post* station WFBE—began airing Reds games. He made household words of "bam" and "whammo" and became the first to scream, "It's going, going, gone," (which he later set to music) when a homer was hit. "Socko!" was another of his favorite expressions, recalled Allen, who worked many years in the Reds' front office.

"Harry was a real character. He used to broadcast in his undershirt while smoking a cigar named Black Peter, which was one of his sponsors. Most of his sponsors were on the seedy side," Allen said.

"He was a good-natured, energetic extrovert," remembered Red Barber, who eventually would put Hartman out of business. Twice, Hartman was named the nation's most popular baseball announcer, in 1932 and 1936, when he outpolled Barber by 36,000 votes. Hartman died of a heart ailment in September 1956, at the age of 53.

Another sportscasting character during the Hartman era in Cincinnati was Colonel Bob Newhall on WLW. A big-game hunter in Africa, Newhall had started as a baseball writer in 1912, fought in World War I, and began one of the first baseball commentary programs on radio. Sponsored by Mail Pouch chewing tobacco, Newhall would recreate dramatic incidents from remembered ballgames.

For decades, plane travel has been the accepted mode of travel for big-league teams, but it wasn't always that way. Train travel was king for close to 60 years. Newhall was part of the broadcast of the first baseball flight. Newhall was on the ground and Red Barber was in the air, describing the first plane trip ever made by a major-league club, in June of 1934 as the Reds journeyed to Chicago. Barber worked a Pioneer portable shortwave transmitter from the plane.

RED BARBER

 Red Barber: CD 2: Tracks 21-23

Red Barber broadcast the first major-league game he ever saw. It was opening day in 1934, and Barber had just accepted the WLW announcing job for a tidy $25 a week. Larry MacPhail had taken over the financially ailing Reds and hired Barber, despite the fact that Barber didn't even know how to score a game.

Born in February 1908 in Columbus, Mississippi, Walter Lanier Barber grew up in Florida and began his radio career in 1930 on station WRUF while he was a student at the University of Florida in Gainesville. During the fall of 1930, he began broadcasting football, and by 1934 he was hired by Powell Crosley, Jr. in Cincinnati to broadcast the Reds games. (Barber had badgered MacPhail with demo records and resumes prior to landing the job.)

Barber's southern drawl was much different than anything Cincinnati fans were used to, but he became an immediate hit. His first co-announcer in 1934 was L.J. Barnes, and the following year Al Helfer joined him for three seasons. When Helfer departed for New York and a network job in 1938, Dick Bray served as the number two man. Barber, Sam Balter and Harry Hartman all broadcast Reds games on different stations in 1938.

While in Cincinnati, Barber broadcast the first night game in major-league history, on May 24, 1935, at Crosley Field between the Reds and the Phillies. Barber anchored the event on the new Mutual Network. He also announced the first of his 13 World Series in 1935 (joined by Bob Elson and Quin Ryan in the Mutual booth) when Detroit beat the Cubs in six games. MacPhail was so enamored with broadcasting that a special hookup from WSAI, WLW's sister station, was installed that enabled MacPhail to flip a switch in his office

and be on the air instantly to talk baseball.

In 1938, the three New York teams were in the fifth year of a five-year contract that banned big-league broadcasting in New York. When MacPhail joined the Dodgers in 1939, he broke the ban and hired Barber as his broadcaster. The Yankees agreed to broadcast just their home games, hiring Arch McDonald of Washington and a young CBS fill-in announcer named Mel Allen.

Barber won immediate acceptance in New York and copped the 1939 *Sporting News* award as tops in the land. He coined several colorful expressions while in Brooklyn, referring to "rhubarbs" and "catbird seats." One scribe, Richard Hubler, defined several of Barber's phrases in a 1942 *Saturday Evening Post* article. "'The boys are tearing up the pea patch,' meaning a rally is in progress. 'Tied up in a crocus sack,' means that the game is in the bag. 'He swung the gate on him,' refers to a takeout play at second. 'Sitting in the catbird seat,' means sitting pretty."

Barber tallied another historic first by broadcasting the first major-league game ever televised when the Dodgers hosted the Reds on NBC, August 26, 1939. (The rights fee consisted of placing a television set in the press room so that the writers could check it out.) Barber sat in an open booth in the upper deck behind third base, without a monitor. There was one camera along both baselines. Barber interviewed several players, asking Dolph Camilli of the Dodgers to hold up his gigantic hands to the camera.

The public received the experiment enthusiastically, with the TV building at the nearby World's Fair bursting at the seams. Barber televised the opening game of the 1940 season and at least one game a week until the war came. In 1946, Mac Phail, now with the Yankees, sold the first commercial TV baseball rights to the Dumont Network for $75,000.

Red Barber, famed broadcaster and host of Red Barber's Clubhouse.

Practically by himself, Barber educated New Yorkers on the game of baseball. He created fans. A woman who knew nothing about baseball before Barber came running into her parlor carrying a half-peeled potato and a paring knife, listening to an apparent Dodger double play. When Barber described the batter safe at first, beating the relay, she muttered, "Oh well, we got the front man," and ambled back to the kitchen.

Barber left the Dodgers in 1953 and joined Mel Allen and Phil Rizzuto on Yankee broadcasts until his firing in 1966.

Al Helfer (left) introducing the new voice of the Brooklyn Dodgers, Red Barber.

Dodger broadcasters Red Barber and Connie Desmond flank owner Branch Rickey in Ebbets Field, 1947.

Red Barber interviews Leo Durocher before the first-ever televised major league baseball game on August 26, 1939.

CONNIE DESMOND

 Connie Desmond: CD 2: Tracks 17, 46-48

Red Barber's partner in Brooklyn for many years was Connie Desmond, who, many thought, rivaled Barber in ability. But alcoholism plagued him throughout his career, limiting his great potential.

Desmond began his broadcasting career on January 20, 1932, on his Toledo, Ohio hometown station, WSPD. At first he used his singing ability and introduced dance band remotes, but he dreamed of following in the footsteps of his idol, Ty Tyson. He never missed a Ty Tyson Tigers broadcast.

"After I'd been on WSPD a few years, General Mills, makers of Wheaties, launched a big baseball sponsorship campaign," said Desmond. "They bought up the rights to every organized league in baseball. It meant about 60 announcers had to be hired. Wheaties planned to broadcast about 25 Toledo Mud Hens games, and I volunteered for the job." He fought his way through the first year, and by the second year, when 40 games were scheduled, he had fallen in love with baseball broadcasting.

After a few more seasons in Toledo, General Mills promoted Desmond in 1940 to broadcast the games of the Cardinals' top farm team, the Columbus Red Birds, on WCOL in Columbus.

"My timing was perfect, because in the two years I was there, Columbus was Little World Series champions and at a peak of prosperity. The pitching staff alone had Harry Brecheen, Preacher Roe and Murray Dickson," Desmond said. The Red Birds' manager, Burt Shotten, would later manage the Dodgers in Brooklyn, with Desmond in the broadcast booth.

In 1942, while in spring training with the Red Birds, Desmond was offered and accepted a job as Mel Allen's partner on the home games of the Yankees and Giants on station WOR. "I was flabbergasted," said Desmond, who was now in the big leagues. "Mel was a treat to work with.

In our first year the Cardinals beat the Yankees in the World Series, and because of my years on the Cardinal farm in Columbus, I felt I was closer to the Cards than the Yankees."

After one year with the Yankees and Giants, Desmond joined Red Barber on the broadcasts of the Brooklyn Dodgers, replacing Al Helfer, who entered the navy. Because of war restrictions, the Dodgers trained on snowy Bear Mountain near West Point.

The Dodgers had won their first pennant since 1920 the year before—in 1941—but it wasn't until 1947 and Jackie Robinson's rookie season that they broke through again.

"[Dodgers general manager] Branch Rickey had been moved by the contributions and loss of life of Negro soldiers in the war and was compelled by the spirit of the Bill of Rights and fair play," recalled Desmond about Rickey's thought process in the lifting of the color line in baseball.

Desmond watched all the hardships Jackie endured, many of which occurred when the team played games in the South. Desmond couldn't even talk about some of the indignities that Robinson tolerated.

"In retrospect, Jackie was probably the most exciting player I have ever seen in my life," said Desmond. "I had to be on my toes just like a pitcher when Jackie got on base. He was a threat to steal any base, including home. He also had an inherent trait to anticipate whether a hit would be a single, double or triple. If he thought he could take the extra base, he wouldn't slow up at all and hit the dirt at second or third with his familiar slide, which was a thing of beauty."

Desmond's baseball broadcasting career in the big show ended in 1957, the last year the Dodgers were in Brooklyn. He gravitated out of the big leagues and back to his roots in Toledo, where he spent his final years broadcasting minor-league Mud Hens games, still shackled by an addiction to alcohol.

Connie Desmond (left) and Ernie Harwell at Ebbets Field in 1948.

VIN SCULLY

 Vin Scully: CD 2: Tracks 16, 18-20

The other member of the Dodgers broadcasting team in the Jackie Robinson era, dubbed the "Boys of Summer" by writer Roger Kahn, was a young kid from Fordham University who went on to have perhaps the greatest career of any sportscaster in history: Vin Scully.

At the ripe old age of nine, young Scully knew he wanted to announce sports as his life's work. "At that early age I began recreating games off the radio in our fifth-floor apartment," said Scully. "I would holler the running report of the game out the window to the kids down in the alley, where they'd be playing games and drinking soda pop." Being raised near the Polo Grounds meant that Scully was a Giants fan as a youth. So the first time he ever set foot in Ebbets Field was as a major-league announcer.

When he was a baby, his mother had often wheeled him around the campus of Fordham University. Following family tradition, he would one day enroll and pursue his degree there. He first entered Fordham Prep and then Fordham University but left after one year, entering the navy during World War II. After being discharged and upon returning to Fordham, Scully discovered that an FM radio station had been installed on the campus.

"Soon my interests swayed to broadcasting. In fact I concentrated all my efforts into the station, even though I was sports editor of the college newspaper," Scully said. Blessed with a beautiful voice and a great passion for baseball, plus a flair for the dramatic, it was just a matter of time before Scully would broadcast his favorite sport.

With graduation approaching, he sent out more than 150 letters to radio stations from Maine to Florida. "The only one to take an interest in me was WTOP in Washington,

D.C.," he recalled. "So that's where I went. I was a staff announcer and summer replacement man, as I assumed all of the announcing duties for each broadcaster on vacation. This was a tremendous break for a kid just out of college, giving me exposure and experience in every facet of broadcasting from concerts to sports."

Arch McDonald was the top sportscaster in Washington, and he took a liking to Scully. "Many times Arch would do a Senators game at night and not be able to get back to the studio in time for his sports show, so he would have me do it for him," said Scully.

Eventually the summer replacement duties came to an end and WTOP offered Scully a permanent job, but not until the following spring. They told him to go back to New York and cool his heels until the call came. But soon a call came from CBS. The network needed an announcer in a hurry to do the 1949 Boston University-Maryland football game. Scully recalled, "Red Barber called me about the job. I got it and began an association with one of the finest men I have ever known." He did one more game for CBS, Harvard-Yale, before going back to "staying alive" and waiting for the WTOP call in the spring.

About a month later, Ernie Harwell, who had been doing the Brooklyn Dodgers games with Red Barber and Connie Desmond, left to join the New York Giants broadcast team. This created an opening, and after much deliberation, Red Barber decided that a young announcer might fit the bill perfectly.

"He wanted someone who wouldn't have his ego knocked about when it came to doing the menial tasks such as gathering lineup cards and scorer rulings. Luckily Red remembered me," continued Scully, "and had me come in for an interview with Dodger boss Branch Rickey. The

A young Vin Scully, who has been broadcasting for more than 50 years.

agreement reached was that I would go to spring training on a one-month option. Either I make it, or they could lose me in the Everglades." That was 52 years ago and Scully has been broadcasting Dodgers baseball ever since.

In sizing up his veteran broadcast partners, Scully, whose hair was redder than "Red's," felt they complemented each other well, despite being from different backgrounds.

"Connie was a Midwesterner, a big easy-going jolly guy with the greatest laugh and a wonderful personality. Red was easy-going, too, but in a Southern sort of way. As he grew older, he became more serious. I was the baby of the bunch. Connie would sit on one side of me and Red on the other, and I'd try and absorb as much of their knowledge as possible."

What Scully needed most, he admitted, was

someone to calm him down when he was trying too hard and to tell him not to be afraid of a little dead air.

"Red and Connie were the best things that could have happened to me," he said. "I was not interested as much in what they said, or how they said it, but *when* they said it. They would often keep quiet and let the crowd roar, which is a marvelous sound, much better than someone saying, 'Gee, what a great play.' The noise from the stands speaks for itself. The greatest bit of advice I ever received was from Red, who told me, 'Don't listen to other announcers and other games, not because you couldn't learn from them, but because you might subconsciously borrow one of their traits. The more you borrow, the less there is of the original product.'"

The eight years Scully spent with the Dodgers in Brooklyn have been romanticized and woven into baseball

Vin Scully (left) with longtime partner Jerry Doggett.

folklore. The players stayed together year after year: Jackie Robinson, Duke Snider, Pee Wee Reese, Roy Campanella, Gil Hodges, Carl Furillo, Don Newcombe, Carl Erskine, and Clem Labine. Ebbets Field was a compact ballpark that brought the fans close to the action. "Broadcasting in that atmosphere was a dream come true for me," said Scully.

The first year he was with the Dodgers in 1950, they lost the pennant in the tenth inning of the final game of the season. The second year they lost it in the bottom of the ninth in the third playoff game with the Giants after Bobby Thomson's memorable home run off Ralph Branca.

"You can't cut it much finer than that. The most pleasing thrill I had in my years in Brooklyn was doing the final four and a half innings of the last game of the 1955 series when Johnny Podres shut out the Yankees."

When Don Larsen pitched the only perfect game in World Series history against the Dodgers the following year in 1956 (one of three perfect games Scully has broadcast), Scully found the game relatively dull. "The Dodgers were being held hitless, and my mind was completely occupied with the thought that the ball club was traveling to Japan immediately after the series was over."

Being born and brought up in New York City, Scully hated the move to Los Angeles after the 1957 season. "Everything that I held close to me was in New York. I had been somewhat of a success in New York, but I didn't know what was in store for me on the West Coast. I went full of misgivings, but I'm delighted with the move today."

Scully has seen both the game of baseball and the philosophy of the broadcaster change dramatically since he broke in.

"Ted Husing had a great vocabulary and Bill Stern was very dramatic, but no one felt they actually knew them. The fans who listen to an announcer today feel much closer to him because of the conversational manner he projects," Scully said.

Scully isn't a fan of the athlete-turned-sports announcer. "I'm glad I broke in when I did and not today. It's come to the point where you have to win 25 games or bat .300 to even qualify as a sports announcer." He also objects to the networks supplying their own announcers to do the postseason, denying the team announcers what to them is the supreme moment of their careers. In a monument to both his durability and his longevity, not to mention his great ability, Scully has broadcast a record 25 World Series and 12 All-Star games.

His ability as a wordsmith and his flair for the dramatic have been heard countless times during some of baseball's great moments, such as Scully's description of Don Drysdale's record for consecutive scoreless innings pitched on June 8, 1968:

"June the 4th he had to go after Hubbell's record, and he beat Pittsburgh five-nothing—and now he's a strike away. The pitch, outside, ball one. The groan from the ballpark. One and two on Roberto Pena. One-nothing Dodgers but right now at 8:45 p.m. that's not the important thing. Drysdale into his windup ... the one-two pitch to Pena, swung on and lined foul into the crowd in back of the Phillies dugout. Still, one-two on Pena. Drysdale takes a break and walks in back of the rubber. They have taken down the 56 on the message board. They would like to change that, so the board is black and waiting. The one-two pitch to Pena. Swung on! A ground ball wide of third. It's Boyer who has the chance. HE'S DONE IT! (crowd roar) ... Don Drysdale has done it and goes back to work."

Twenty years later, in 1988, Scully would broadcast the feats of Orel Hershiser, who pitched 59 consecutive scoreless innings, breaking Drysdale's record of 58 2/3.

Scully has been blessed with great health and enthusiasm to sustain the rigors of travel and broadcasting a 162-game schedule for more than 50 years. The key to his longevity stems from his broadcasting philosophy.

"Even though the travel is demanding, I've never grown tired of broadcasting major-league baseball. I've never once tried to pawn myself off as a baseball brain or the sport's foremost authority. I'm not interested in a golden microphone resting on my tombstone. On the contrary, I'm just a fellow doing a job, and if I get stuck or make a mistake, I'll be the first to make it known."

MEL ALLEN

 **Mel Allen**: CD 1: Track 24

Over in the Bronx, in the Yankees' broadcast booth, sat Mel Allen. "How about that?" Allen, like Barber, was from the South, and he was Barber's biggest competition on the major-league broadcasting stage. Allen began announcing the home games of the Yankees and Giants in 1939, switching exclusively to the Yankees in 1946. He remained through the 1964 season, which produced the last Yankees hurrah after an amazing dynasty that saw the Bronx Bombers win five consecutive world crowns from 1949 through 1953 and a host of other pennants and championships.

Mel Allen was born Melvin Israel on Valentine's Day, 1913, in Birmingham, Alabama. His father's dry goods business had the family on the move from town to town before Papa Israel sold the business and settled in Greensboro, North Carolina. It was there that young Melvin became the batboy of the minor-league Greensboro Patriots.

Entering the University of Alabama at the age of 15, Allen remained there eight years, graduating with a law degree in 1936. His first announcing job was doing the public address for Alabama home football games in 1934. Impressed with Allen's expertise on the microphone, Crimson Tide coach Frank Thomas recommended Allen to a Birmingham radio station. Soon after, in 1935, he was hired to broadcast Alabama and Auburn home games for $5 a game.

After two years as Alabama's football announcer, Allen, still known as Mel Israel, took a trip to New York City to see the bright lights. Out of curiosity he walked into the CBS building and asked if he could audition for an announcing job. To his surprise, he was offered a part-time job with the CBS network. Thinking it would last about six months, whereupon he would return home to begin a law career, Mel accepted the job. After just two months, however, he was taken off staff announcing duties and made the understudy of Ted Husing and Robert Trout, the two most eminent broadcasters in their fields, sports and news. About this time he dropped the last name Israel and adopted his father's middle name, Allen.

His big break in radio occurred when he covered the Vanderbilt Cup auto race from an airplane. "We flew round and round, but nothing happened," remembered Allen. "I could see the cars lined up, but the weather was bad. Because of a steady downpour, I ad-libbed about an hour on a race that never materialized." Allen's 52 minutes of ad-libbing convinced the CBS brass to give him a shot as a sportscaster.

Soon more opportunities came, including the 1938 World Series broadcast with France Laux and Bill Dyer, despite the fact he had never broadcast a major-league game. In 1939, he began announcing the home games of the Yankees and Giants with Arch McDonald, who had left the Washington Senators play-by-play job to try his luck in the Big Apple. Allen was supposed to swap with Arch and move to Washington, but the Senators' owner Clark Griffith surprisingly hired immortal pitcher Walter Johnson to broadcast his team's games instead.

Allen didn't join McDonald until six weeks into the season when General Mills decided to bounce Garnett Marks from the broadcast and replace him with Allen as McDonald's assistant. Then McDonald lasted only one season in New York with his homespun, countrified delivery, and returned to Washington, leaving Allen as the chief announcer. Actor J. C. Flippen assisted Allen in 1940 and Connie Desmond came aboard in 1942.

After a stint in the army in which Bill Slater, Don

Mel Allen in 1938.

Dunphy and Al Helfer broadcast the games, Allen returned for good in 1946, beginning a stint of 19 seasons as the voice of the Yankee dynasty. In 1967 he televised the games of the Cleveland Indians, and in his twilight years he found fame with a new generation of fans as the voice of the weekly TV series, *This Week in Baseball*.

Allen admitted that his famous home run call, "Going, going, gone," came about quite by accident. "Sometimes people in our profession will deliberately try and think of something clever. 'Going, going, gone,' came about when a player hit a long drive and I wasn't sure if it was gone. I hesitated, watching the outfielder drift back. I said 'Going.... Going,' and when the outfielder gave up and it sailed over the fence, 'Gone.' The phrase stuck with me for 23 years."

Of all the games he broadcast, he ranked Don Larsen's perfect game in the 1956 World Series as his top thrill. Allen broadcast the first half and Bob Wolff announced the second half.

"I broadcast the first half of that game but was just another fan during the second half. It was the first time I can recall myself becoming emotionally involved in a sports event. I was rooting so hard I broke a blood vessel in my

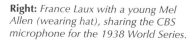

Top: *Mel Allen behind Babe Ruth in 1947 on Babe Ruth Day. Ford Frick is on the left and Cardinal Spellman next to Allen.*

Right: *France Laux with a young Mel Allen (wearing hat), sharing the CBS microphone for the 1938 World Series.*

throat and when I went to broadcast my nightly report on ABC, I could hardly talk. But it was worth it. The game was a once-in-a-lifetime event," Allen said.

Perhaps the most touching event Allen covered was Babe Ruth's farewell at Yankee Stadium on June 13, 1948. His throat ravaged by cancer and his once-ample body wasting away, Babe stood with tears in his eyes as the crowd stood and applauded. Allen went up to the Babe.

"I asked the Babe if he wanted to say anything. 'I must,' he replied. In a faded and raspy voice, the great Bambino spoke, not of past glories but of the nation's youth and what the world offered for them. There wasn't a dry eye in the house, mine included."

Fittingly, in 1978, Mel Allen and Red Barber were the first broadcasters inducted into the broadcaster wing at the Hall of Fame where they each received the Ford C. Frick award.

Allen passed away on June 16, 1996 at the age of 82.

ARCH MCDONALD

Arch McDonald, who lasted just a year in New York, was probably the best known sports voice in Washington history, broadcasting Senators games from 1934 until his untimely death in 1960, excluding the one season in New York.

He began his career in Chattanooga with the Lookouts, the Senators' top farm team, and was voted the most popular minor-league announcer in 1932 by *The Sporting News*. When he began with the Senators, he handled only the telegraphic recreations of the road games, except for opening day. Using his theme song, "The Old Pine Tree," which he sang on every broadcast, Arch quickly won over the Senator fans with his brand of hillbilly humor and down-home philosophy.

Wrote *The Sporting News* upon his winning the outstanding baseball announcer award in 1942: "McDonald can emit a more sorrowful banshee wail when a player hits into a bases-loaded double-play. And he can whoop it up like a holy roller when Washington runs are crossing the plate."

In 1935, a portable broadcasting booth was installed in the new downtown Peoples Drug Store in Washington, and Arch soon had an average of 300 onlookers on hand as he recreated road games. In 1937, General Mills and station WJSV in Washington sent McDonald to the Senators' training camp in Orlando, Florida, and with the use of a 1,000-mile direct wire—the longest yet used for daily programming—Arch became the only announcer in spring training to broadcast on a live, daily basis.

The native of Hot Springs, Arkansas, was not an overnight success. Before radio, he spent years as a roustabout, butcher, ham actor, oil rigger, soda jerk, refrigerator salesman, second in Jack Dempsey's corner, and fight referee. When he got the PA job with the Lookouts, team owner Joe Engel quickly had him doing games on radio. Wrote J.G. Taylor Spink upon Arch's selection as 1942 announcer of the year: "No textbook equipped McDonald for the task of regaling the American public with his tales. No rules of syntax cramp his style. The mountain folk of his native South gave him his idioms. A cowhand of the Panhandle left a word with him that pops into the microphone at the correct moment. "They Cut Down the Old Pine Tree" became the song of the city. When Arch walked into public places, the orchestra struck up the tune. Members of Congress hummed it. At times fans wanted to wrap up Clark Griffith's Senators in that casket of pine, but Arch's wisecracks and droll condonings of diamond atrocities laughed them out of mayhem and the like."

Arch McDonald died of a heart attack while playing bridge on a train that was returning from the Redskins-Giants game on October 16, 1960. The game had ended in a thrilling 24-24 tie. On his final weekend on Earth, he was doing everything he enjoyed. He had broadcast the Maryland football game on Saturday, the pro game Sunday, and was engaged in his favorite pastime, bridge, when the end came.

Arch McDonald (left) with Russ Hodges in the late 1930s.

Top: *France Laux (left) and Arch McDonald talk baseball in 1942.*

Right: *Arch McDonald (left), Red Barber, and Walter Johnson in April 1939.*

Top: *Arch McDonald, on the occasion of his being named broadcaster of the year by The Sporting News in 1942. Longtime Washington reporter Shirley Povich is in the middle and France Laux on the right.*

Left: *Arch McDonald and Bobby Feller in 1936.*

BOB WOLFF

 Bob Wolff: CD 2: Tracks 26, 27

Bob Wolff began as Arch McDonald's assistant in Washington and became the chief announcer upon McDonald's death. The Duke graduate began his career on campus station WDNC while a sophomore in college. After the war, in which he wrote training books and films, he became Washington's first TV sportscaster. At the age of 24 he was telecasting Senators baseball, launching a 14-year career with the club.

With the Senators perennially in the cellar, Wolff made a goal of being fresh, novel and entertaining.

"I've broadcast several memorable games that got very few headlines and were only viewed by a few thousand people. But emotionally, these games were as important to me as a coast-to-coast network assignment," Wolff said.

Echoing many other broadcasters, Wolff said that Don Larsen's perfect game was one of his top thrills. "Working with the Senators didn't give me a shot at many national assignments but my efforts doing the 1956 All-Star game in Washington paved my way to the series and perhaps the most dramatic World Series game of all time." Wolff said he only mentioned the no-hitter at the end of an inning. "I didn't want to be commenting on a perfect game at the precise moment someone gets a hit. The audience would be screaming 'Doggone it, why didn't Wolff keep his mouth shut?'"

Wolff was also fortunate enough to broadcast the Colts-Giants NFL sudden-death championship game in 1958, called "The Greatest Game Ever Played."

Wolff accompanied the Senators franchise when it moved to Minnesota in 1961, teaming with Halsey Hall, and when Lindsey Nelson left NBC to join the Mets in 1962, Wolff replaced him on the NBC *Game of the Week* telecasts with Joe Garagiola in 1962, 1963 and 1964. He then joined Madison Square Garden Corp. as a vice president in charge of broadcasting.

Game of the Week baseball announcers Joe Garagiola and Bob Wolff in 1964.

AL HELFER

 Al Helfer: CD 1: Tracks 30, 31

Al Helfer got his nickname, "Mr. Radio Baseball," from his five years broadcasting Mutual's *Game of the Day*. It was a grueling five years, broadcasting a different game in a different city every single day—a routine that his doctor eventually convinced him to give up.

"The *Game of the Day* was the brainchild of Paul Jonas, once a song plugger but then the sports director of the Mutual Network," said Helfer towards the end of his long career. "On a July afternoon in 1949, I was at the Polo Grounds getting ready to broadcast a Giants game when I met Paul, who knew my wife, the piano-playing Ramona of Paul Whiteman's orchestra, who had played some of his tunes when he was in the music business.

"'I think,' Jonas told me, 'that I've talked the network into trying the first coast-to-coast daily broadcast of major-league games.' Unlike the Liberty Network, which recreated the action, these would be live broadcasts. This entailed having two crews in different cities, in case of rain, and a lot of air travel."

Jonas offered Helfer the top announcing job on the *Game of the Day*, and Helfer accepted. Art Gleeson, later the sports director at Mutual, and ABC announcer Gene Kirby joined Al on the main broadcast team. At one time there were 686 stations in the United States carrying the *Game of the Day*, plus stations in Canada, Mexico, South America and overseas, bringing the total up to 1,490 outlets. "In the five years, I think my crew missed only three games," remembered Helfer. "That meant flying three times in a day in the era before jet travel. Finally, after five years, under doctor's orders, I resigned, even though I loved the job and loved the title 'Mr. Radio Baseball.'"

Helfer's broadcast career began in 1932 on station WWSW in Pittsburgh. Born and raised 30 miles southwest of Pittsburgh in the Monongahela valley, Helfer played football and basketball at Washington & Jefferson College in nearby Washington, Pennsylvania, where he also headed the sports department of the local radio station, WMBO. After graduation he took a job with the *Pittsburgh Post-Gazette* as a cub sports reporter and broadcast the football games of the Pitt Panthers and Carnegie Tech on the paper's radio station, WWSW. "In 1933 the station decided they wanted to announce baseball games," recalled Helfer. "At that time there was a ban on airing a game live from Forbes Field, so announcers Lewis L. Kauffman of station KQV and Tony Wakeman were recreating the games. I did the same thing on WWSW in 1933 and 1934. Even though Pie Traynor and the Waner brothers were still playing, the Pirates were a second-division club by that time."

During those recreations, Rosey Rowswell would often sit in with Helfer, serving as a color man, which was a great help because of the lulls in the game. "When I left Pittsburgh, Rosey asked me if I'd recommend him as my replacement. The station liked his homey style, and he became an instant fixture," Helfer said.

Gaining experience and crafting his own announcing style, Helfer departed Pittsburgh in 1935 to join Red Barber on the broadcasts of the Cincinnati Reds on station WLW. "Red and I clicked right away, and it was a thrill to actually be broadcasting from a ballpark and not a studio. Larry MacPhail was running the club and on May 24, 1935, we broadcast the first major-league night game, won by the Reds 2-1 over the Phillies. The crowd was over 20,000—ten times larger than they'd have drawn in the afternoon."

Helfer departed Cincinnati in 1937 to join CBS in New York and announce primarily football. He broadcast a few select baseball games in 1937 and 1938 from Yankee Stadium to see if attendance would fall off like the owners predicted. The games were a big hit, and when Larry MacPhail took over the Dodgers in 1939, he broke the ban.

"MacPhail wanted the same broadcast crew he had in Cincinnati, so Red called me in New York and said, 'What do you say we get back together and give 'em hell in Brooklyn?' 'Let's go, I'm ready,' I told him," Helfer said.

The success of the Dodgers broadcasts translated to increased crowd totals, and soon the Yankees and Giants worked out a deal with General Mills to air their home games. "They tried to get me to quit the Dodgers and head the Yankees-Giants crew, but Red and I wouldn't split," recalled Helfer. Red and "Brother Al" functioned well together on the Dodger broadcasts, but it wasn't to last very long because of World War II.

As a naval officer, Helfer helped lead the 1943 Allied invasion of Sicily, known as Operation Husky. "In less than two days we put over 80,000 men and 8,000 vehicles on the island, and not without stiff resistance. The *Cavalcade of America* radio program dramatized our landing a few years later, with Alfred Drake playing the part of Lt. Commander Helfer, which was a proud moment in my life. I've done many things in my life that I never started out to do and that I wouldn't want to do again, but I wouldn't take a million dollars for having gone through them. Because of what we were fighting for, my military career was one of them."

Red Barber wanted Helfer to rejoin the Dodgers broadcast team after the war, but Connie Desmond was then well established, and Helfer refused. Connie had gone to Dodgers management on his own, offering to step down, but Helfer didn't want to hamper Connie's position with the Dodgers. Instead, he joined Bill Slater for one year doing the Yankees and Giants home games and then freelanced until he began the *Game of the Day*.

When he left that job for medical reasons after five years, Walter O'Malley, the Dodgers' owner, asked him to come back to Brooklyn, where he worked with Vin Scully and Connie Desmond until the Dodgers headed west. Electing not to move to Los Angeles, Helfer took on a host of assignments, including televising Phillies games back to New York to see if there was interest in plugging the gap left by the Dodgers' and Giants' moves. He also televised games from Havana, Cuba, and in 1960 and 1962 worked the first season of the expansion Houston Colt '45s. When the Oakland A's headed west from Kansas City in 1968, Helfer came back after a five-year hiatus to team with Monte

Moore and announce for Charlie Finley. He retired for good after the 1969 season.

In recounting his memorable moments behind the mike, Helfer started with the 14 no-hitters he broadcast in the major leagues, the last being Jim "Catfish" Hunter's perfect game in 1968 against the Twins. It was the first perfecto in the American League since 1922.

"I remember the thrill of seeing Allie Reynolds, Bob Feller, Ewell Blackwell, Tex Carleton, Johnny Vander Meer and Carl Erskine, who tossed two no-hitters. I broadcast Vander Meer's second consecutive no-hitter on June 15, 1938, on the occasion of the first night game in Ebbets Field history. Johnny walked the bases loaded in the bottom of the ninth, and Red and I were hanging limp in the booth. Next came a forceout at home on a ball hit to Lew Riggs at third and finally Leo Durocher popping up to Harry Craft in short center to end it."

Helfer passed away on May 16, 1975 at the age of 63.

Al Helfer, Mr. Radio Baseball, broadcasting the Mutual Game of the Day in the early 1950s.

JIM BRITT

Jim Britt: CD 2: Tracks 35-37

Jim Britt was nicknamed "Brittle Bones Britt" because by the time he was 31, he had already busted, fractured, chipped and dislocated more than 200 bones, and the end wasn't in sight.

The voice of the Boston Braves and Red Sox had physical problems from a young age. Born in San Francisco, young Jim's family moved to Erie, Pennsylvania, Baltimore and Denver by the time he was 11. From age 11 to 25, he lived in Detroit.

"After being injured playing football, baseball and basketball, I could scarcely play any sport, except golf, and even it took a couple of blows at me," remembered Britt. "Once, when I was playing a match as a member of the University of Detroit golf team, I broke my left hand for the 16th time." The reason for the brittle bones? When he was 14 he contracted rheumatic fever, which seemed to break down the strength in his bones.

His entry into broadcasting came quite by accident. A prelaw major at Detroit, Britt listened to a 1933 broadcast of a Titans football game and thought the announcing horrendous, which he relayed to coach Gus Dorais when he bumped into him the following week. "You think you could do a better job?" asked Dorais. "How could anyone do a poorer one?" Britt answered.

A few days later Dorais called Britt and asked him to take over the announcing job. "But Gus, I've never broadcast a game before in my life," Britt told him, startled by the offer. "Well, you weren't kidding me when we met the other day on the street. I dare you to do it." The next week Britt was broadcasting Detroit football.

"The dare was the only reason I consented to broadcast the remainder of the schedule, because I didn't receive any money for doing the games," he added.

At the University of Detroit, while studying for his law degree, Britt also captained the debate team and taught debating, public speaking and dramatics in the Detroit school system. He sang with different orchestras in Detroit and secretly aspired to become a crooner. He soon tired of law school. After getting married, he quit school and sold insurance, which he didn't like any more than law.

In 1935 Britt got his first paying job on radio. Unbeknownst to him, Gus Dorais and Ty Tyson recommended him to a small station in South Bend, Indiana, home of the Fighting Irish of Notre Dame, where Dorais had starred several years before. His starting salary was $50 a week, a huge sum of money in those depression times. "My big duty was to broadcast Notre Dame football," said Britt, who took the examination that all football referees had to take, "not that I had to, but I wanted to know as much about the game as the fellows that handled it or played it."

His great memory of Notre Dame football was broadcasting the fabled 1935 clash between the Irish and the Buckeyes of Ohio State in Columbus. "Both Grantland Rice and Warren Brown, two respected sportswriters, came on with me at halftime," recalled Britt. "Ohio State led 13-0 at halftime and Granny offered hope to the kids on the Notre Dame campus, and sure enough Notre Dame pulled off a miracle and won 18-13."

One night in 1937, Britt got a call from Russ Hodges, who was working at WIND in Gary, Indiana, telling him about a job opening at WBEN in Buffalo.

"I got the job and soon was doing telegraphic recreations of Buffalo Bison games. Roger Baker was the big name in Buffalo sports broadcasting when I arrived. The first

Jim Britt, who was the announcer of the Army All-Star football games in the early 1940s.

time I did a telegraphic recreation in competition with Roger, I finished the Buffalo-Syracuse game 20 minutes before he did. He was allowing for Western Union misadventures while I just plunged in," laughed Britt, whose only experience doing recreations had been some Notre Dame basketball games.

The first two no-hit, no-run games Britt ever broadcast, he didn't see. They were recreations of Johnny Vander Meer's back-to-back no-hitters against Boston and Brooklyn. He was sitting in the Statler Hotel in Buffalo, recreating big-league games on nights when the Bison weren't playing.

It was while in Buffalo that Britt made up his mind that he was going to broadcast major-league baseball, and in 1940, when Frankie Frisch left the Boston radio booth to manage the Pirates, he got his chance. Frisch, who announced one year, and Fred Hoey were the only baseball announcers Boston had until he arrived.

"Ted Williams was in his second season when I arrived in town, and anyone who didn't see greatness in Ted as a young hitter, even at a young age, was in the wrong pew. The only pitcher that gave Ted much trouble was Satchel Paige," said Britt. "Ted saved his pennies to watch Satchel barnstorm in San Diego, and when he was inducted into the Hall of Fame he implored baseball to recognize the greats of the old Negro Leagues, which of course they eventually did."

Britt witnessed the hatchet job done on Williams by the Boston press. "It wasn't all the writers, just two or three in Boston. They went to the park hoping Ted would have a bad day. Otherwise they wouldn't have a column."

In the early 1940s, Britt's boss on the Yankee Network, John Shepard, sold a 15-minute *Superman* show over the network from 5:15 p.m. to 5:30 p.m. "Every day we had to suspend the game for the Superman break, and if the game was still being played at 5:30, we'd come back on. Otherwise we'd just recap the missing minutes. This went on for a full season," marveled Britt. "You can imagine how the fans reacted when the count was 3-2 on Ted Williams with the bases loaded and out blared, 'It's a bird! It's a plane! No, it's Superman!'"

Britt was one of the few broadcasters to serve two teams at the same time, so he was often accused of being both pro-Braves and pro-Red Sox. "I subscribed to Ty Tyson's advice, 'Report the game, don't play it.'"

But others appreciated his descriptive efforts.

"Not so long ago," reported the *Boston Post* on Britt in 1941, "he received a letter from a blind man who he made the game appear so realistic to him. In the letter the blind man wrote, 'When you yelled "duck" as the foul came towards the mike, I actually fell on the floor.'"

After he broadcast the 1942 All-Star game from the Polo Grounds, Britt received papers ordering him to active duty as an army lieutenant. On the last day of the season, instead of signing off with his trademark phrase, "Remember, if you can't take part in a sport, be one anyway, will you?" he said, "If you can't take part in the war, buy bonds anyway, will you?"

Britt was in air intelligence in the Pacific.

"It spared me from hitting the beaches in a landing barge, but I was in enough places to remember how scared I was." One narrow escape involved a midair plane crash out of Tarawa to drop bombs over Japan. His plane managed to limp back to the base along with seven others. Six people were killed.

After his discharge in 1946, Jim broadcast his first World Series on the Mutual Network as the Red Sox lost to the Cardinals in seven games. His partner was Arch McDonald from Washington. His first broadcast partner in Boston was Tom Hussey, and after Tom departed, Britt worked with Bump Hadley, Leo Eagen, Bob Delaney and Lester Smith, among others. In 1949 he televised the first World Series upon the joining of the coast-to-coast cable. "I tried to let the picture tell the story. Because I did it that way, Sid Gross, a New York writer, wrote a critique saying I didn't talk enough. About three years later I televised a Sugar Bowl game, and Gross again wrote a column, this time saying I was 'talk-talk.' So there was no way I could win."

Britt's most memorable interview? It was with famed writer Henry McLemore. "Near the end I asked him what was his favorite sport. He answered calmly, 'You mean outside of rock climbing?' 'I mean, what's the greatest spectacle you've covered in your years as a sportswriter?' I persisted.

"'That's simple,' replied Henry. 'An America's Cup yacht race.' And as he raised his drink to his lips, he muttered, 'The particular one I covered, I got up at 5 o'clock in the morning with a hangover and looked out the window into a dense fog and watched two boats sail off in opposite directions.' There was only one Henry McLemore."

In 1951, when the two Boston teams began airing their road games, Jim had to decide which team he would broadcast, the Red Sox or the Braves. "I picked the wrong horse and chose the Braves, while Curt Gowdy was hired by the Sox. Just two years later Braves owner Lou Perini moved the club to Milwaukee, shocking all of us, including Warren Spahn, who was building a restaurant across from Braves Field. I didn't follow the club to Milwaukee."

Wrote Jerry Nason in the March 20, 1953 edition of the *Boston Globe*: "Whether you listened to Jim Britt or turned him off, he has left his mark on this town. The tremendous effort he made for the Jimmy Fund [helping children with cancer] and the magnificent new hospital building for which he was in large measure responsible is the monument he leaves behind."

Britt had a particular memory of broadcasting Braves baseball. "In 1946 I was forced to swallow one of my pet phrases describing a home run, 'There goes one clear out of the park. That's one ball we won't see again.' Bill Nicholson of the Cubs hit a long drive that bounced off concrete to the right of the jury box, and I said 'That's one ball we'll never find.' When I left the park, I noticed three or four policemen standing around my 1946 convertible. Upon reaching the car I noticed a shattered hole in the windshield and Nicholson's ball resting on the front seat amidst a pile of glass."

After a few years broadcasting football games for NBC, ABC and Dumont, Britt landed in Cleveland where he telecast Indians games from 1954 through 1957 before an eye injury forced him to give up play-by-play broadcasting. "If there was any acid in his cup, he swallowed the bitter brew in silence and sang no sad songs. The bloke had gutsy gumption," wrote Austen Lake in the *Boston Record American* in 1963 after Britt returned to Boston to do some freelance work. "He still shows the old sterling character. And it also demonstrates how expendable a public figure can be in a brief eye flicker. And also how brief is public gratitude."

Britt died on December 28, 1980 at the age of 70.

The first Boston baseball telecasting team started in the 1947-48 season. They were Tom Hussey (right) Jim Britt (middle) and former Yankee pitcher Bump Hadley.

KEN COLEMAN

When Curt Gowdy left the Red Sox to broadcast major events for NBC in 1966, Ken Coleman was picked to replace him. A New Englander by birth, growing up near Boston in Quincy, Coleman had become a favorite in Cleveland as the TV voice of the Indians and the Browns. One of the cool veterans of the profession, Coleman admitted to being too frightened to accept his first offer in broadcasting, even though he had dreamt of becoming a sportscaster since the age of nine, when he listened to Fred Hoey doing the Red Sox and Braves games.

"I was 18 and in the army in the China-Burma-India theater of war, when a chance came to announce sports for the Armed Forces station in India. I turned it down," winced Coleman, "because the thought of speaking into a microphone with 12,000 troops listening frightened me greatly. This bothered me, and upon release from the military I entered Curry College in Boston where I overcame this fear."

After a year at Curry, Coleman joined WSYB in Rutland, Vermont, broadcasting Northern League baseball for the Rutland Royals, whose star pitcher was 16-year-old future major-league pitching star Johnny Antonelli.

In 1952 Coleman got his big break when he was picked by head coach Paul Brown to be the television voice of the Cleveland Browns, an association that lasted for 14 years. Two years later he also joined the Indians' TV network in their pennant-winning year to begin a 10-year association.

"Paul Brown insisted I live like the players at training camp, in a Hiram College dorm room," recalled Coleman about the innovative Cleveland coach.

"It was Paul's idea that if I was going to broadcast Cleveland Browns football, I should learn as much about the team as I could. It was a great education and one of the best breaks I ever had. I knew a little about football, or I wouldn't have gotten the job, but by the time that 1952 training camp ended, I think I could have become a coach."

Coleman, who still dabbles in broadcasting in the Boston area, announced some memorable moments in both baseball and football. The Cleveland Browns were at their zenith when he broadcast their games, culminating with the 1964 NFL championship win over the Baltimore Colts.

He also announced Ted Williams's 500th homer on a misty night in Cleveland; Early Wynn's 300th victory, after several unsuccessful tries, on a hot muggy night in Kansas City; Rocky Colavito's four-home-run performance in Baltimore on June 10, 1959, a feat accomplished just twice previously in American League history; the Indians' doubleheader sweep of the Yankees in 1954 before more than 86,000 fans that all but clinched the American League pennant for the Indians; and the Impossible Dream season of 1967 in which the Red Sox, a tenth-place finisher the year before, "rode the greatest single season performance I have ever seen by a ballplayer, Carl Yastrzemski, into the American League pennant," Coleman said.

"Yaz won the Triple Crown, going seven for eight in the last two games of the season, which the Sox needed to win to at least tie. The seasons come and go and you remember the high spots. Pushed into the corner are the lonely days and nights in hotel rooms and all the weeks away from home. Tension and pressure on a daily basis, but it was a privilege being part of it."

Ken Coleman

HARRY CARAY

 Harry Caray: CD 2: Tracks 10, 11

A broadcaster is lucky if he makes a mark in one community, let alone two. Harry Caray became a legend in two towns, St. Louis and Chicago, with three different teams. Four, if you count the old St. Louis Browns. Baseball was nothing but a big party to Harry, a stage that saw him become bigger than some of the teams he talked about. He truly loved the game, and he truly loved life, and when he died at 83 on February 18, 1998, he left the city of Chicago and the game of baseball in mourning.

His trademark phrases of "Holy cow!" and "It could be—it might be—it is!" were part of the St. Louis summers for 25 years. Incredibly, after Gussie Busch fired him in St. Louis and he bounced back to work for Charlie Finley in Oakland in 1970, he landed in Chicago where he would spend another 27 years broadcasting for the White Sox and finally for his beloved Cubs at Wrigley Field. "Let me hear you!" Caray would scream as he leaned out of his booth at Wrigley Field, ready to lead the crowd in the seventh-inning singing of "Take Me Out to the Ballgame." "He was beyond an icon, beyond an ambassador of the game," said the Cubs' then first baseman Mark Grace after Caray's death. "He was the most popular figure in the game, without a doubt."

Wherever Caray went, and a great portion of his day was spent leaning against a bar where the drinks were on him, he was on center stage. Pete Vonachen, his friend for almost 50 years and owner of the Peoria Chiefs Midwest League club, said that "the secret of being Harry's friend was having a cast-iron stomach, endless stamina, keep your bags packed and your divorce lawyer on retainer."

None of the broadcasters in this historical retrospective have had to combat greater odds to rise to the top. There was no silver spoon in Caray's mouth at birth. He was born Harry Carabina in a poor, tough neighborhood in St. Louis where his father died when he was an infant and his mother died of cancer when he was nine, thus thrusting him into a series of foster homes. Broadcasting was the last thing on his mind as a youngster. To him, it was a profession reserved for college grads and men of letters. The first time broadcasting entered his mind was in high school. He was playing amateur ball and dreaming of the big leagues. After graduation, knowing his limitations as a player, he thought more and more about announcing baseball.

Upon his graduation, Caray wrote a letter to Merle Jones, the general manager of KMOX radio, which broadcast the home games of the Cardinals and Browns. The letter actually was more about the way the games were being broadcast than anything he might offer as an alternative. He did say, though, that he could do a better job than the popular veteran France Laux. Because of the brash nature of Caray's letter, Jones contacted him and offered him an audition.

The audition script ran the gamut from news to musical names such as Puccini and Beethoven, which were completely foreign to Caray. He took it home, practiced diligently and returned to KMOX for his tryout. Jones wasn't there when he auditioned, and "after I stammered and stuttered my way through the copy, the program director gave me the old song and dance about starting on a smaller station and coming back in a few years." Caray countered by telling the program director that Mr. Jones wanted to personally hear his audition and that he would abide by whatever Mr. Jones told him. "It was a one in a thousand shot, but I told him I wasn't going to leave until I saw Mr. Jones," recounted Harry. "As it turned out, Mr. Jones hadn't

Harry Caray

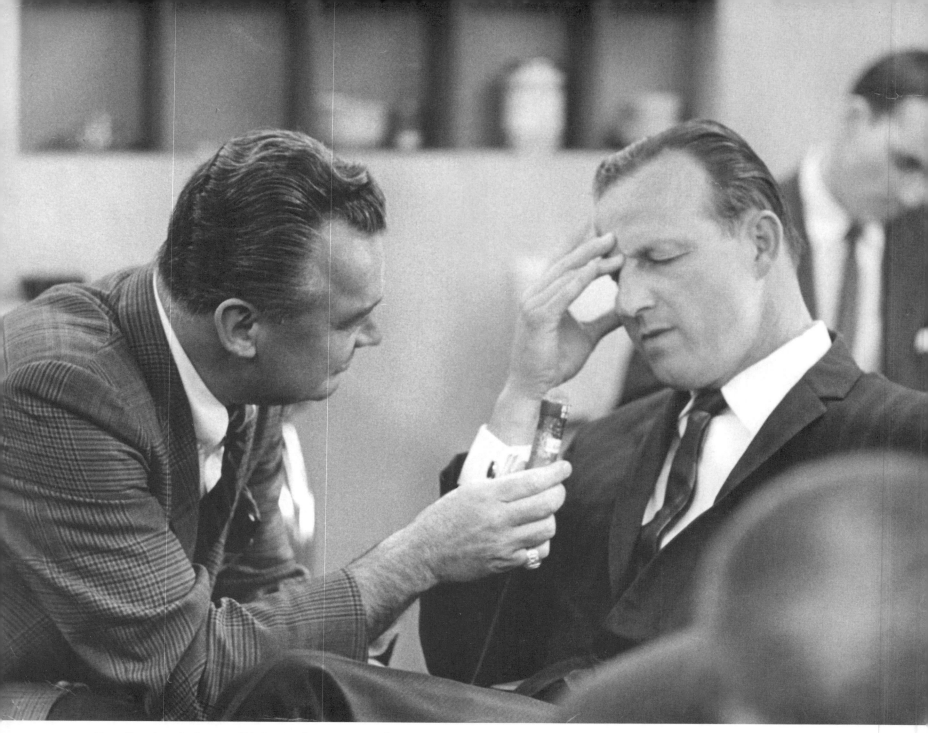

Harry Caray interviewing one of his favorite players, Stan Musial.

been informed about my audition, and he gave the program director some grief. It was decided I would have another audition, this time with Mr. Jones in the audience."

Harry was more confident and relaxed the second time through, and Mr. Jones was impressed with the quality of excitement in his delivery. "He promised to help me all he could, saying he'd contact his friends at smaller stations, and if I was willing to go anywhere, I'd get an opportunity. As it turned out, I landed in Joliet, Illinois, where I went to work as an all-purpose sportscaster."

He gained vital experience in Joliet by recreating Cubs and White Sox games. Then, after a year and a half, he joined WKZO in Kalamazoo, Michigan, which was owned by John Fetzer, the future owner of the Detroit Tigers. He was only there a year before moving back to St. Louis, because he was married with a child and thought he'd be entering the military.

Weak eyesight kept him out of the service, however, so he took a job as a staff announcer at KXOK in St. Louis. "After about a month, I talked my boss into letting me do a nightly sports show, which was radical for the times because I editorialized frequently, interjecting my own opinions," said Caray. More and more people began listening to the brash young newcomer.

At about that time, the Griesedieck Brothers brewery obtained the contract to sponsor the baseball broadcasts of the Cardinals and Browns. The year was 1945, and the brewery went in search of a broadcaster. Other broadcasters, such as Laux, were connected with other breweries, and as the search wore on, the brewery kept hearing the name of Harry Caray pop up. "They had already hired a number two man, former catcher Gabby Street, and thought I'd fit the bill of a number three man. I quickly tried to convince them that I should be the number one man," Caray said.

Caray made his pitch, saying that since Griesedieck was new to baseball, a fresh new personality with a novel style was what was needed. In short, himself. But they were uncertain about Caray's unorthodox style. "I'll never forget Mr. Griesedieck saying, 'You know, what I like about France Laux is that I can read the newspaper and still listen to the ballgame.' I shot back, 'If you can do that, then you're wasting all that money on advertising, because no one is listening.'"

Harry Caray with Cardinals third baseman Ken Boyer.

Griesedieck blinked once or twice, looked at Caray, and said, "Young man, you have something there. I think we'll take a chance with you."

Caray and Gabby clicked immediately as a team. "I could see a wealth of information that could be gleaned from Gabby, if he was used properly. I had a beautiful relationship with him. He was the closest thing to a father I knew, since my dad had died when I was an infant. He had his own way to personalize and recount a story, always from true life and always with a philosophical message. If I did anything for Gabby, it was to give him the opportunity to relay to the public some of the insight he had never been given the

Harry Caray with Curt Flood.

opportunity to reveal before. Instead of commenting on the obvious, I was able to lead him into the anecdotes that were on the tip of his tongue."

The Cardinals were one of the great franchises when Caray began as their broadcaster in 1945. Stan Musial, Enos Slaughter, Terry Moore and Marty Marion were the nucleus, with Red Schoendienst joining the club the same year Caray did. Harry Brecheen, Murray Dickson and Howie Pollett anchored the pitching staff.

In the 1940s, if it wasn't the Cardinals, then it was the Dodgers, vying for the top. Caray remembers when Jackie Robinson joined the Dodgers in 1947 and came to play the Cardinals for the first time. "Just before the Dodgers came to town, someone sent a letter to the Cardinals' president, Fred Saigh. The letter, which I wasn't aware of, stated my life was in danger and Sportsman's Park would be blown up if Jackie set foot on the field. Saigh gave the letter to the FBI, but not before the story leaked to the newspapers."

Caray was coming out of a movie house when he heard the newsboys shouting, "Read all about it! Harry Caray gets death threat!" Caray immediately ran over and bought a paper, in shock because this was the first he had heard about the threat. Two policemen accompanied him wherever he went at the park, and nothing, fortunately, came of it, but it did illustrate the racial unrest present when Jackie Robinson broke the color line.

In 1946, Caray and Gabby began recreating Cardinals road games because of the hot pennant race, often abandoning the Browns' home games. Using sound effects and a lot of poetic license, the Caray-Street team took off in popularity. For months people thought they were actually at the park, even though they announced at the outset that they were not. The recreations were scrapped at the tail end of the 1948 season, and in 1949 the two broadcasters began traveling with the Cardinals. Street passed away in 1951 and was replaced by another former catcher, Gus Mancuso.

Then in 1952, Anheuser-Busch bought the Cardinals, which placed Caray's job in jeopardy. The consensus was that because of his nine-year association with Griesedick, he would be replaced. Instead, the opposite happened. Gussie Busch wanted Caray to remain and offered him a two-year contract, which he accepted.

What Gussie didn't tell Caray, however, was that he wanted him to take a year off to indoctrinate himself with Anheuser-Busch. Busch didn't think Caray could stop talking about Griesedieck beer after nine years and suddenly begin plugging Budweiser. Caray devised a survey that asked whether Harry Caray should continue as the Cardinals' announcer or be replaced. It came out in his favor, which proved he was more identified with the team than the beer. Mancuso was let go and Jack Buck and Milo Hamilton came aboard for a season, to be followed by Joe Garagiola the next year.

Caray formulated his broadcasting style as a carryover of his personality as an excitable, passionate person. "Every pitch to me is a thrill," he said. "Every play has its own individuality. I don't fake excitement. The public is too smart for that."

The question of "impartiality" was one of Caray's pet peeves. "Every time I see the word, I seem to be the one it's referred to, sometimes in a deprecating manner. If you mean I favor my own team and discolor the accomplishments of the opposition, then you are wrong. Many fans in St. Louis felt I gave too much credit to the opposition."

His philosophy was simple. He thrilled at the beauty of a play no matter who made it, and he would honestly be lost without a baseball game to broadcast. Caray never lost his enthusiasm for the game. It was as if each time he was walking into the ballpark it was for the very first time, and he was enthralled by the game and its players.

When he began in radio in the early 1940s, his style was totally different than the calm, mellow-toned, matter-of-fact style of the time. His sponsors even thought he was too radical, but that soon changed as his popularity grew. As one newspaper put it, "If you lack the tickets to see the Cards, you can listen in your own backyards, and the greatest show, no ifs or buts, is to hear Harry Caray going nuts."

As a youngster, Caray always thought that if you didn't smoke, you would be a better athlete and that if you didn't cuss, you would be a better man. "Out of desperation not to use profanity, I began saying 'Holy Cow!' And when I used it on the air, the phrase really caught on. For years I got mail addressed only to 'Holy Cow.'"

His audience was both fanatical and widespread, off

the powerful signal of KMOX, which under ideal conditions could be heard in 14 states and on a network of 124 stations in those states. Caray was powerful, and over the years he drew the wrath of managers and players alike as being a "rip artist." Caray said that the truth hurts and that players and managers (he had a long-running feud with Eddie Stanky) deserving of criticism should be criticized. "I refuse to fool the audience," he stressed.

His home run call also became one of his signatures. "When a long fly ball is hit, I automatically begin saying, because I am so closely on the play, 'It might be…it could be…IT IS!' These were the three levels of development which I connected to a home run. Rather than wait until the ball lands in the seats, I wanted to bring the true picture of the moment to the fans."

Following the career of Stan Musial was an immense thrill for Caray. "I don't think Stan has ever made a mistake on the field or off it. He's been successful in everything he ever approached. That old cliche, 'Being a credit to the game,' should be expanded to 'a great credit to manhood,' when the name Stan Musial is mentioned. He epitomizes the best of everything a person can be. Baseball always makes the individual, except in Stan's case. He helped make baseball the great game it is."

Caray proved his toughness in early November 1968, when he was hit by a speeding car while crossing the street in downtown St. Louis. The impact threw him 35 feet into the air. He suffered compound fractures of both legs, a compound fracture of his right shoulder, head and chest injuries and deep facial cuts. He nearly bled to death on the street, but he defied his doctors and was back to normal a few months later. On opening day, Caray was given a huge ovation as he walked out on the field, dramatically shedding a pair of canes as the crowd went wild.

"Lying in the hospital I had much time to reflect," remembered Caray, "and for the first time in my life I learned humility. I had over 300,000 pieces of mail from total strangers and over 85,000 mass and prayer cards. For the first time in my life I realized that I was blessed with the opportunity to extend a service to the public that I had never realized. I was stupid, unaware of the effect I had on other people, absolute strangers. It made me feel very warm inside."

He was fired after the 1969 season by Busch (there were reports of a dalliance between Caray and one of the Busch family wives), and his firing sent tremors through the Midwestern plains and left him reeling for a while. "I actually wondered during the winter just what my reaction would be when announcing for a team other than the Cardinals, because I loved them so. But as much as I love them, I realize now that it is primarily the game itself that I love even more."

Caray spent the next year in Oakland, getting along fine with Charlie Finley but clashing with incumbent announcer Monte Moore. He lasted just one year there before moving back to Chicago, flip-flopping with Bob Elson and joining the White Sox in 1971, single-handedly jump-starting baseball on the south side.

Things really got wild when Bill Veeck bought the White Sox, for he was almost as crazy as Caray, who did many broadcasts shirtless from the center-field bleachers, surrounded by fans, near an outdoor shower and a barber chair. Caray's broadcast partner, the colorful former outfielder Jimmy Piersall, provided more comic relief, and like Caray, he pulled no punches if a player deserved criticism, rankling players such as Richie Zisk.

In 1982, Caray took his show to the north side and Wrigley Field, where he became as familiar as the ivy-covered walls, using his fishnet to snare foul balls and leading the crowd in the singing of "Take Me Out to the Ballgame" during the seventh-inning stretch.

Caray always felt that announcing baseball was like being in show business, because the announcer brings the life of a play into the listener's living room. The degree by which he accomplishes the transfer of action from field to living room separates the good announcer from the mediocre one.

"I don't subscribe to the theory that the game itself is enough to sustain the audience. I compare it to the theater. If the actor doesn't have a feel for the part he's playing, the play could flop even though it's a literary masterpiece." And for more than 50 years until his death in 1998, Caray played his role in Oscar-winning form.

Harry Caray and Cardinals and Browns co-voice Gabby Street around 1945.

JACK BUCK

 Jack Buck: CD 2: Track 12

Like Harry Caray, who broadcast over both radio and television with aplomb, Jack Buck was equally adept behind the mike or in front of the cameras. For 15 years, the glib, quick-witted Buck backed up Caray in St. Louis, and when Harry departed, he moved into the top job where he remained for another 35 years.

Buck was born in Holyoke, Massachusetts, the third of seven children. His father had been a great athlete at Holyoke High, pitching a perfect game and garnering a tryout with John McGraw's Giants before taking a job with the Erie Railroad.

A Holyoke pharmacist, for whom Jack ran errands, took Buck to his first big-league game. They traveled 90 miles to watch the Red Sox play Cleveland in a Fenway Park twin bill. "I had already begun switching my allegiance to Cleveland since my father had just been transferred there, but the Indians dropped both ends. I also made it to the 1935 All-Star game in Cleveland, sitting in the bleachers, where Jimmy Foxx socked one of the longest balls ever hit in the Cleveland stadium. Up to that time, I thought that day was the greatest I had ever experienced."

After high school graduation in Lakewood, Ohio in the late 1930s, Buck bounced from the ore boats of Lake Erie to the battlefields of Europe as an army infantryman in the famed 9th Infantry Division. In March, 1945, he was among the first to cross the Remagen Bridge, spanning the Rhine, as the Allies pushed into Germany for the final drive of the war. "A few minor charges exploded as we were going over, but we captured the span intact, thereby wiping out Hitler's last natural stronghold in the west."

As the 9th Infantry smashed into Hitler's Third Reich, Buck was hit, wounded in the left arm. He was released from a LeMans hospital the day the war ended, May 8, 1945, and was able to join in the wild celebration. "I still believe," he said decades later, "that the most interesting aspects of my life, outside of sports, were working on the ore boats and my army career. So many things happened in those two endeavors that helped to form my character. I came so close to dying so many times that it's a wonder I'm still around."

Right around the age of 16, Buck began thinking about eventually becoming a sportscaster. One of the reasons was that he felt he could do a better job than some incumbent broadcasters. He loved Bob Elson in Chicago and Jack Graney in Cleveland but wasn't that hot about Ty Tyson and Harry Heilmann in Detroit. After the war Buck worked on all sorts of jobs, from restaurants to riveting. He worked for Midland Steel and Glidden paints and was learning how to be a crane oiler, pile driver and steel hoister when he ran into a fellow who was headed for Ohio State and needed a roommate. This was a Saturday, and classes began on Monday.

"I had planned to go to college sometime, and because of the G.I. Bill, tuition wasn't a problem. So I dropped everything and went," said Buck. He had no papers and hadn't even applied. But determined to enroll, he made out a schedule and went to classes. "The professors always wondered who I was, and many tried to throw me out of class, but I told them to hold off until my papers arrived. After awhile they grew weary and just ignored me."

Buck enrolled in 1946 and by 1948 was doing sports on the campus station, WOSU. One afternoon he

Jack Buck

was working in the newsroom when someone mentioned an opening on one of the commercial stations in Columbus, WCOL. "Don't bother to apply, Buck, because I've already been down there," said a coworker. To a man like Buck, who had to scratch and work for everything he got, that was like waving a red flag in front of a bull.

"Just before going to work at my all-night gas station job, I called WCOL and got the name of the general manager," remembered Buck. "His name was Ed Sprague. I wasted no time, calling him at home and arranging for an audition the following day. I skipped a few classes, went to WCOL, auditioned, got the job and was on the air at 5:30 that evening."

For $5 a show, Buck did an early evening and a late night sports show. The first event he ever broadcast was an Ohio State-DePaul basketball game on WCOL. From there, he auditioned for Columbus Red Birds general manager Al Bannister. "I sat in one room talking into his intercom while he sat in another room with a group of advertising clients," said Buck. "He handed me a copy of the 1949 *Sporting News* baseball guide which contained in the back a summary of the 1948 World Series. I auditioned by recreating a game from the guide and was able to get through it without a major mishap." He got the job. Within months he was doing Red Birds games, Ohio State football and basketball and several sports shows a day.

Buck broadcast Red Birds baseball in 1950 and 1951. Rollie Hemsley managed the 1950 team that beat Baltimore to win the Little World Series. The following year it was the other extreme. Under Harry Walker, the Birds lost 101 games. Buck learned a lot that season. "When you're losing twice as many games as you're winning, you have to work extra hard," he said, "and I was doing the games by myself, doubleheaders and all." In 1953 Buck left WCOL and the Red Birds to join the new TV station in Columbus, WBNS, where he did a sports show as well as a morning variety show. His most embarrassing moment in broadcasting occurred at WBNS. "I had a TV show called *Buck Eyes Sports*, and Earl Flora, then the sports editor of the Ohio State *Journal*, had a show called *Florascope on Sports*," recalled Buck.

"My show was seen at 5:30 p.m., and Earl was at the tail end of the news and weather, about 6:20. One night I did my show, went home—which was 15 minutes from the station—and flipped on the TV to watch the news, weather and sports. When it came time for Earl's show, the announcer came on and said, 'It's time for *Florascope on Sports*, and here substituting for Earl Flora is—Jack Buck.' Well, I was sitting home sipping a beer watching this thing, and I have never experienced a feeling before or since quite like the one I felt at that moment. Here I had forgotten all about filling in for Earl, which I had agreed to do. The next thing the announcer said was, 'One moment please.' A TV station is so busy at that time of night, no one paid any attention to the fact I wasn't there. It's just taken for granted that everybody is there. Well, I was absent that night, and what transpired in the boss's office the next morning makes me again feel lucky to be alive."

At about that time, Rochester's minor-league club was looking for a broadcaster. Bing Devine, the Red Wings' general manager and future Cardinals general manager, called Al Bannister in Columbus in search of an announcer. Bannister called Buck, who by this time was a father of two and living in a two-room apartment.

"I drove to Rochester, a Cardinals farm team, and met Bing, and within minutes I became the voice of the Red Wings." The Red Wings' sponsor was Old Topper beer, but Old Topper wasn't around long, as Anheuser-Busch had just bought the parent team Cardinals. So Budweiser replaced Old Topper as Red Wings sponsor."

This change in beers led to Buck's first major-league job in St. Louis in 1954. "Throughout the '53 season I had kept after the Cardinal brass, letting them know who I was and where I was. I did what amounted to a live audition when the Cardinals decided to televise nine out-of-town games back to St. Louis with nine different announcers auditioning live." Buck was one of the nine, broadcasting the St. Louis-New York Giants game at the Polo Grounds, and once again he got the job.

Harry Caray had been beating the drum for Chick Hearn to move from Los Angeles to St. Louis, but Hearn turned it down, enabling Buck to get his first big-league opportunity with the 1954 Cardinals. But in 1956, Buddy Blattner was hired to do the telecasts, and Buck was fired. He quickly joined ABC and did the *Game of the Week* before being rehired by the Cardinals for good in 1957. "Before I was fired I was being paid as the number two announcer.

When I came back it was for a larger salary and the option to do football and other sports. Getting fired is usually good for you," Buck surmised. The year with ABC led to his telecasting AFL games when the league debuted in 1960.

As far as memorable baseball seasons, the 1964 season ranks at the top of Buck's list. "Not only because the Cardinals overtook the collapsed Phillies for their first pennant since 1946, but because of all the things that happened that year," remembers Buck. "Bing Devine, the man who gave me my early break, was fired as general manager. Manager Johnny Keane was on the ropes all season and finally quit after the World Series, replacing Yogi Berra [as the Yankees manager] and then dying a short time later, perhaps of a broken heart."

The day the Cardinals clinched the pennant by beating the Mets on a Sunday afternoon, where was Buck? He was doing the Bears-49ers game at Kezar Stadium, broadcasting the play-by-play while listening to the Cardinals game by phone.

"I would have hated to be tuned into the football game that afternoon with 'the bases loaded, third and three,'" laughs Buck. "I wonder how many mistakes I made that day. I would've enjoyed so much being with the Cardinals on that final Sunday, and that's why I relished the 1967 clinching in Philadelphia, even though they threw me in the shower, dumped a bucket of ice over my head and ended up ruining a $200 watch. It was a small price to pay."

Several more World Series teams followed in St. Louis, and with the heroics of Mark McGwire, Buck has added to his memory book a thousand fold. In 1987 Buck was paid the ultimate compliment for his announcing skills by being inducted into the broadcasters' wing of the Baseball Hall of Fame as the recipient of the Ford C. Frick Award. In 1998 the Cardinals honored Buck by unveiling a bronze sculpture of him outside Busch Stadium's main ticket lobby. For a kid who became a man on the ore boats of Lake Erie, it couldn't get much better than that.

Buck died on June 19, 2002 at the age of 77.

Jack Buck (left), former player Heine Meine and France Laux on a 1956 TV show in St. Louis.

RUSS HODGES

 Russ Hodges: CD 2: Tracks 1-5

October 3, 1951. It's a date engraved in sports history. A benchmark of baseball history. It's the day Bobby Thomson hit the "Shot Heard 'Round the World," the three-run homer off Ralph Branca that lifted the Giants over the Dodgers to the National League pennant.

Over on 12th Street in Brooklyn that afternoon, the Lawrence Goldberg family was fiddling with a brand new tape recorder. Someone suggested taping the final innings of the Dodgers-Giants playoff clincher at the Polo Grounds. The three-game series was tied at one game apiece, and the Dodgers led 4-1 heading into the bottom of the 9th inning. The Giants were in a tough spot, but adversity was nothing new for Leo Durocher's Giants. After all, they had trailed Brooklyn by 14 games in mid-August.

The Giants rallied in the 9th. Whitey Lockman doubled in a run with a solid hit to the left-field corner, sending Don Mueller to third. Mueller severely sprained his ankle sliding into third and was replaced by Clint Hartung. Before the next batter, Bobby Thomson, stepped to the plate, Dodger skipper Charlie Dressen strode to the mound. After meeting with Don Newcombe, Pee Wee Reese, Jackie Robinson and Rube Walker, Dressen summoned right-hander Ralph Branca from the bullpen.

There were other broadcasts of the game on local radio, including the Dodger station with Red Barber, Connie Desmond and Vin Scully, but the Goldbergs were tuned into Giants broadcaster Russ Hodges, and this is what they heard:

"A home run would win it and a single would more than likely tie up the ballgame and keep the inning going.

Branca's on the spot and he knows it. ... Hartung down the line at third, not taking any chances. Lockman with not too big a lead at second but he'll be running like the wind if Thomson hits one. Branca throws. THERE'S A LONG DRIVE; I BELIEVE—THE GIANTS WIN THE PENNANT, THE GIANTS WIN THE PENNANT, THE GIANTS WIN THE PENNANT, THE GIANTS WIN THE PENNANT— THOMSON HIT IT INTO THE LOWER DECK OF THE LEFT-FIELD STANDS—AND THEY'RE GOING CRAZY! I DON'T BELIEVE IT. I WILL NOT BELIEVE IT. BOBBY THOMSON HIT A LINE DRIVE INTO THE LOWER DECK OF THE LEFT-FIELD STANDS AND THE PLACE IS GOING CRAZY. ... AND THEY'RE PICKING UP BOBBY THOMSON AND CARRYING HIM OFF THE FIELD. OH BABY!"

The Goldbergs, along with the rest of New York, sat stunned and motionless listening to the drama emanating from the Polo Grounds. Lawrence Goldberg, a waiter in a restaurant, switched off the tape machine, not knowing that he had been the only person to record Hodges' thrilling play-by-play description. Not even the flagship station WMCA had recorded it. Hodges had given a fleeting thought to wishing he had a copy of the broadcast but had already inquired, and the engineer said there was no copy.

Fortunately for Hodges and baseball fans everywhere, Goldberg had taped it, and he got in touch with Hodges that night to let him know. Over the years that broadcast became synonymous with baseball history and with broadcaster Russ Hodges. A record album, sponsored by Chesterfield cigarettes, was put out with the exciting last few innings.

Hodges had taken over the Giants' radio

Russ Hodges, behind the CBS mike in 1949.

Russ Hodges worked for the Mutual Broadcasting System from 1942 to 1945.

Russ Hodges in 1969.

microphone in 1949 after assisting Mel Allen on Yankees broadcasts since 1946. Larry MacPhail was still running the Yankees in '46 and called Hodges in Washington to offer him a job. At first Hodges thought it was a crank call, but once he realized it was MacPhail, it didn't take him long to accept the offer and head north to New York City.

Early in that 1946 campaign, in which the Yankees finished far behind the Red Sox, the Indians came to Yankee Stadium, and Bob Feller, back from military service, was pitching like the prewar Feller. He was no-hitting the Yankees. Hodges had broadcast two no-hitters while with the White Sox, one by Vern Kennedy and the other by Bill Dietrich, but Mel had never broadcast one. "I had been taking the third and seventh innings and Mel was handling the rest," recalled Russ. "But I could see the delight Mel was having and so I told him before my turn in the seventh, 'I've had no-hitters before; you see if you can get one.' It was a thrill for Mel, and that night at Toots Shor's, he told columnist Bill Corum that I had relinquished my turn so that he could complete the game. Corum thought enough of my gesture to write about it in his next-day column, which I still treasure."

In 1949 Giants owner Horace Stoneham gave Hodges "a job for life," to replace Frankie Frisch, who returned to the field as a coach, giving up the microphone. "Leo Durocher had replaced Mel Ott as manager," said Hodges, "and Leo began dismantling a power-laden club of Johnny Mize, Willard Marshall and Sid Gordon. He made a big deal with the Braves, trading Marshall, Gordon, Buddy Kerr and Sam Webb and acquiring Alvin Dark and Eddie Stanky. The Braves wanted young Bobby Thomson, but Leo convinced them to take Marshall."

By 1951 the Giants were contending, and in May of that season, when Willie Mays was promoted from Minneapolis, they jumped a few notches higher in stature. "I remember Willie's first at bat in the Polo Grounds," recalled Hodges. "He homered off the first pitch Warren Spahn served up. Since then I'm the only man alive to have seen every one of Willie's homers."

Even with Mays's rookie heroics, the Giants still trailed the Dodgers by 13 1/2 games on August 11, 16 in the loss column. Then came a phenomenal 16-game winning streak that trimmed eight and a half games off the lead in

less than three weeks. "Leo had become a wild man," said Hodges, "and his team fought and gnawed and clawed its way closer to the top. Still, though, it was going to take a miracle for the Giants to win the pennant."

The Giants were four and a half games down with ten to go but swept the Braves to close the gap to two and a half with four to go. New York journeyed to Boston to close out the season while the Dodgers had a half-game lead and finished with three games in Philly. "The Phillies beat Brooklyn in their first game while we were idle," remembered Hodges, the emotion still there some 20 years later. "That made it all even with two games to go. Sal Maglie beat the Braves the following day while the Dodgers beat the Phillies, setting up a dramatic final day. Larry Jansen polished off the Braves 3-2. We hung around as long as we could listening to Braves announcer Jim Britt recreating the Phillies-Dodgers game. When we caught the train, the Phillies led 8-5, and we thought it was over. The champagne bottles were ready to be uncorked on the ride home. I found a phone on the train and called WHN in New York, the Dodger station. I began calling the play-by-play to the Giants. We never popped the corks, as Jackie Robinson homered in the 14th to win 9-8, forcing a playoff."

Moments like 1951 are what kept Hodges going. Long air flights, all-night coffee shops, middle-of-the-night hotel check-ins and upside down sleeping schedules were part of the negative side of the business. Born in Dayton, Tennessee in 1910 and raised in Danville, Kentucky, Hodges was fanatical about sports from an early age, serving as the water boy to the famed football "Prayin' Colonels" of Centre College, who, led by Bo McMillan, sprang several major upsets in the 1920s and captured the nation's fancy. "My father was a telegrapher for the Southern Railroad," recalled Hodges, "and we would head north whenever he got a promotion, all the way to Cincinnati, so in a nutshell my childhood was woven along those railroad tracks."

Offered a football scholarship at the University of Kentucky, Hodges suffered an ankle injury in his first game as a sophomore. That injury paved the way to a career in radio.

Hodges spotted for announcer George Wederhold, who was announcing the Kentucky-Tennessee game on WHAS in Louisville. Wederhold's knowledge of football

was hazy at best, and he asked Hodges to broadcast the second half. That was the start. His career in railroading was over before it started.

From those humble beginnings, Hodges joined WCKY in Cincinnati on a part-time basis while attending law school at night. After graduation in those tough Depression times, he discovered there wasn't much demand for lawyers, so he cast his lot with radio, broadcasting the Reds games directly from the park for $25 a week in salary.

"Larry MacPhail arrived in Cincinnati in 1933, and he brought in Red Barber from Florida to do the games, and suddenly I was on the outside looking in," said Hodges.

He took a job on WHBF in Rock Island, Illinois, where he did minor-league baseball and Iowa football. Ralph Atlass, who ran station WIND in Chicago, twisted his dial one Saturday afternoon and came across Hodges doing an Iowa football game. His baseball announcer, Johnny O'Hara, was in the process of moving to St. Louis, and Atlass was looking for a replacement. He wired Hodges on a Sunday evening, asking him to come to the station in Gary, Indiana for an audition.

"I beat Mr. Atlass to his office the next day," said the eager Hodges. "I was sitting in the lobby by the time he got to work. I accepted the job that morning without even inquiring about salary." Hodges did Cubs and White Sox home games, Big Ten football and boxing.

In 1938, when WIND began broadcasting horse races and dropped baseball, Hodges landed in Charlotte, North Carolina, to recreate the games of the Charlotte Senators. His employer was Wheaties, which at that time was trying to make inroads in the South.

Four years later, in 1942, Wheaties transferred Hodges to Washington where he worked Senators baseball, with Arch McDonald, and Redskins football. Then came the call to join the Yankees in 1946 and the Giants in 1949.

After the Giants' sweep of the Indians in 1954, they didn't play in another World Series until 1962. And once again they had to beat the Dodgers in a playoff. The big difference was that the teams were now on the West Coast and not in New York. Performer Danny Kaye made a record spoofing Chuck Hiller, Tom Haller and Stu Miller, all of whom played key roles in the Giants' success. Compared to 1951, there was far less drama this time around.

"Billy Pierce shut out the Dodgers 8-0 to win the first game. The Giants led 5-0 only to see the Dodgers win 8-7 in L.A. in game two. We were three runs down before coming back to win 6-4 in the decider and I screamed just as I did in '51, but this time nobody was cheering since we were at Dodger Stadium. I felt I should have been sad for some reason," Hodges said.

"That 1962 team, even though we lost the series to New York, was the best club the Giants had in my time with them. Billy Pierce, for instance, was a thing of beauty, the dying gasp of a real champion. He was Mr. Clutch, even pitching the last of the ninth in the final playoff game, retiring the side in order."

In 1963, Hodges authored a book on his years in New York and San Francisco. Published by Doubleday, *My Giants* could just as well have been called *Bye Bye Baby*, in tribute to his famous home run call.

Hodges left us much too soon. He was just 60 years old when he died on April 19, 1971.

The path of Bobby Thompson's home run in the October 3, 1951 game that clinched the Giants' pennant win. Russ Hodges announced the game and is famous for his screams of "The Giants win the pennant."

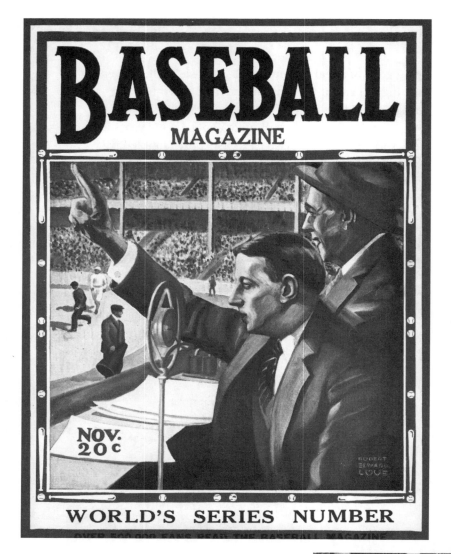

BASEBALL
MAGAZINE

NOV. 20c

WORLD'S SERIES NUMBER

Bases 'n Cases

Vol. 2 No. 8

Published for Baseball Broadcasters by
KNOX REEVES ADVERTISING, INC.
Minneapolis

August 12, 194

4,000 KIDS WITH WHEATIES BOXTOPS ATTEND OKLAHOMA CITY BASEBALL SCHOOL

Pull out that drawer marked "adjectives - for great promotions" and toss them all to Curt Gowdy, KOCY and Oklahoma City General Mills representatives for one of the outstanding promotions of the season.

4,000 kids, each with a Wheaties box-top, stormed the gates of the Oklahoma City park for the Wheaties Baseball School. It was one of the largest and most successful sports promotions ever staged in Oklahoma City.

Curt Gowdy, KOCY and General Mills men started the ball rolling by gaining the complete cooperation of Harlod Pope, President of the Oklahoma City Indians. After obtaining the ball park for the Saturday morning school, a local bottling company and an ice cream company were contacted. 3,000 bottles of pop were donated by the General Beverage Company and 3,000 Eskimo pies given by the Steffen Ice Cream Company - when the crowd went over 3,000 emergency supplies were rushed to the park.

Oklahoma City Indian ball players shared the success as they appeared to give the kids instruction. Al Rosen, sensational young third baseman and leading batter in the Texas

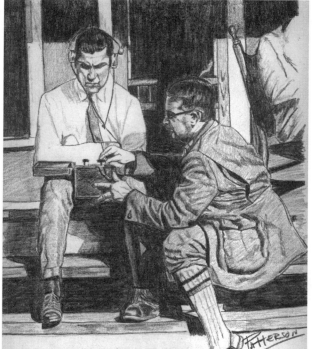

Author's rendering of announcer J. Andrew White and champion Jack Dempsey in 1921.

Log of Play-by-Play Broadcasts, Telecasts

FROM AMERICAN LEAGUE CITIES FOR 1951

CHICAGO	BOSTON	ST. LOUIS	CLEVELAND	PHILADELPHIA	DETROIT	WASHINGTON	NEW YORK

CHICAGO

BOB ELSON
Announcer—
Bob Elson
Stations, kilocycles or megacycles—
WJJD (day)—1160
WCFL (night)—1000
Games—
Home and road
Sponsors—
Sinclair Refining Co.
Goebel Brewing Co.
Television—
WGN, Channel 9
Announcers—
Jack Brickhouse
Harry Creighton
Games—
All home except night
Sponsor—
The American Vitamin Association, Inc.

BOSTON

CURT GOWDY
Announcers—
Curt Gowdy
Robert De Laney
Tom Hussey
Stations, kilocycles or megacycles—
WHDH (850)
WHDH-FM (94.5)
Games—
Home and road
Sponsors—
Narragansett Brewing Co.
Atlantic Refining Co.
Television—
WBZ-TV, Channel 4
WNAC-TV, Channel 7
(Alternate days)
Announcers—
Curt Gowdy
Robert De Laney
Tom Hussey
Games—
All home
Sponsors—
Atlantic Refining Co.
Naragansett Brewing Co.

ST. LOUIS

HOWARD WILLIAMS
Announcers—
Howard Williams
Bud Blattner
Stations, kilocycles or megacycles—
KWK (1380)
Games—
Home and road
Sponsor—
Falstaff Brewing Corp.
Television—
KSD-TV, Channel 5
Announcers—
Howard Williams
Bud Blattner
Games—
Selected games as TV facilities permit
Sponsor—
Falstaff Brewing Corp.

CLEVELAND

JIMMY DUDLEY
Announcers—
Jimmy Dudley
Jack Graney
Al Hoegler
Stations, kilocycles or megacycles—
WERE (1300)
WERE-FM (98.5)
Games—
Home and road
Sponsor—
Standard Brewing Co.
Television—WXEL
Channel 9
Announcers—
Hal Newell
Larry Allen
Games—All home plus few road games where cable lines are available
Sponsor—
Leisy Brewing Co.

PHILADELPHIA

BYRUM SAAM
Announcers—
Byrum Saam
Claude Haring
Ray Walton
Stations, kilocycles or megacycles—
WIBG—990
WIBG-FM—94.1
Games—All
Sponsors—
Atlantic Refining Co.
P. Ballantine & Sons
Supplee-Wills-Jones Milk Co.
Television—
WPTZ, Channel 3
(Saturdays)
WFIL-TV, Channel 6
(Weekdays)
WCAU-TV, Channel 10
(Sundays)
Announcers—
Saam and Haring
Games—
All home except night
Sponsors—
Atlantic, Ballantine

DETROIT

HARRY HEILMANN
Announcer—
Harry Heilmann
Stations, kilocycles or megacycles—
WJBK—1490
WJBK-FM—93.1
Games—
Home and road
Sponsor—
Goebel Brewing Co.
Television—
WWJ-TV, Channel 4
Announcer—
Harry Heilmann
Games—
35 selected dates
Sponsor—
Goebel Brewing Co.

WASHINGTON

ARCH McDONALD
Announcers—
Arch McDonald
Bob Wolff
Stations, kilocycles or megacycles—
WWDC—1260
Games—
Home and road
Sponsors—
Christian Heurich Brewing Co.
Sinclair Refining Co.
Television—
WTTG, Channel 5
Announcers—
Arch McDonald
Bob Wolff
Games—
21 selected dates
Sponsor—
Christian Heurich Brewing Co.

NEW YORK

MEL ALLEN **ART GLEESON**
Announcers—
Mel Allen and Art Gleeson; also Dizzy Dean and Bill Crowley on network.
Station, kilocycles—
WINS—1010
Games—Home and road except only day games on network
Sponsors—
P. Ballantine & Sons
General Cigar Co.
Network Sponsors—
P. Ballantine & Sons
Atlantic Refining Co.
Television—
WABD, Channel 5
WPIX, Channel 13
Announcers—
Mel Allen, Art Gleeson, Bill Crowley and Dizzy Dean.
Games—
WABD—All home except night
WPIX—All home games
Sponsor—
P. Ballantine & Sons

EXTRA INNINGS

As the 1930s unfolded, it was evident that radio broadcasting had made an unmistakable impression on the world of sports. That a fan in Buffalo could find out the outcome of the World Series as soon as the man whose apartment window overlooked Yankee Stadium was almost incomprehensible. People who never before took an interest in sports found them to be entertaining and exhilarating.

Many listeners never knew what was involved in a baseball game until radio brought the living voices and actions of the players into their living rooms. Women who once scorned boxing found themselves standing on chairs during the excitement of the Dempsey-Firpo fight. People listened to an event one day and found themselves wanting to be there in person the next. Before the broadcasting of the 1922 and 1923 World Series, the parks were filled only on occasions—such as the deciding game—but after radio began relaying the action direct, attendance and gate receipts soared.

The Baseball Writers Association of America had initially objected to the World Series broadcasts on the grounds they would hinder the sale of papers that carried game stories. Instead, radio helped the sale of papers by the tens of thousands. Many who listened had a desire to read more detail about what had taken place. Radio was building attendance at games and building the circulation of newspapers; across the country several broadcasters were becoming household names in big cities and small towns for their coverage of sports on radio.

The following section highlights some of those well-known names.

"Ty" Tyson frequently worked at the WWJ studios and is shown taking his cue from engineer Ed Boyes.

FRED HOEY

In 1925, Fred Hoey began broadcasting the home games of the Boston Red Sox and Braves on WNAC, the flagship of the Yankee Network, which comprised 22 stations throughout six New England states.

Hoey was a true baseball broadcasting pioneer. Born in Boston in 1885, he began writing schoolboy sports in 1903 and became the chief usher at the old Huntington Avenue ball grounds, the forerunner of Fenway Park, in 1905. He was soon writing baseball full-time, and in his spare time, he was responsible for helping to make professional hockey possible in Boston. He was a player, coach, referee, manager and publicity director at the old Arena, and when the Bruins arrived in 1924, he joined them as publicist, all in his spare time. He was regarded as "Mr. Hockey" in New England.

Hoey was a technician on the radio, completely detailing every play while keeping his language simple and understandable. In 1931 the fans tendered Hoey a day at Braves Field, and more than 30,000 admirers came out to honor him. There was a move by the fans in 1931 to have Hoey picked to broadcast the World Series, but by 1933 he still hadn't been selected.

Wrote noted Boston columnist Bill Cunningham in August, 1933: "They don't broadcast games in New York, which is one reason for Gotham's interest in Fred, since they pull in Braves and Red Sox games from Bridgeport. It's entirely possible that the leagues will vote to ban broadcasts from all their parks, and then the thousands who have become familiar with Fred's pleasant voice and crisp diamond descriptions will be bereft indeed. In the meantime he's the ace of the airwaves, and you're right, he belongs in the World Series spot."

The article must have had some impact, because just a month later Hoey was picked by CBS to announce the first and fifth games of the 1933 World Series between the Senators and Giants. Commissioner Landis had decreed that neither Ted Husing of CBS nor Graham McNamee of NBC would broadcast the play-by-play, since they hadn't done games in the regular season. They were relegated to second banana status, known in today's vernacular as "color."

"I'm tickled to death," said Hoey. "My only hope seemed to be if Boston won, but the fact that both Series teams are from the east and I'm the only broadcaster doing games regularly in the east helped my chances." Landis appointed two minor-league announcers along with Hoey to do the series, Gunnar Wiig from Rochester and Roger Baker of Buffalo.

The eight-year crusade to get Hoey into the World Series took a sudden turn for the worse during the first Series game, when his voice went out. It was impossible to hear him on the West Coast, as his words seemed garbled and jumbled.

All of New England was asking, "What happened to Fred Hoey?" The clear bristling voice they were used to was little more than a whisper, and he was forced to quit after four and a half innings. The story that was reported said Hoey, hoarse with a cold that settled in his throat, insisted on broadcasting the game so as not to disappoint his legion of fans. His doctor, who had been treating him for several weeks, insisted that Hoey stop his pipe smoking, which he refused to do.

In the years that followed, the mystery of the Hoey breakdown continued to be discussed. Some say he was swallowed up by the bright lights of New York and was still in a stupor from the night before. Others said he was kidnapped by rival NBC and fed excessive amounts of alcohol.

Fred Hoey

Said his longtime WNAC engineer Jack Moakley, "There were all sorts of rumors that he had been jobbed by some of the national announcers of high repute. He did lose his voice, and after that he never came to a game without carrying a tin of throat lozenges."

Hoey himself described his embarrassment this way: "Today, unfortunately, my voice cracked in one of the best assignments of my life. Crashed and cracked because of my own fault. I didn't take care of a cold, and I date the trouble to the dramatic six-games-in-four-days series between the Braves and Giants to end the season." Hoey never recovered sufficiently to broadcast again in the Series.

One of Hoey's quirks was mixing up words and letters of words. Said Moakley, "One day, instead of his normal opening, which was 'Good afternoon everybody, this is Fred Hoey speaking,' out of the horn came 'Good afternoon Fred Hoey, this is everybody speaking.' Once, during a close game, Jimmy Foxx crushed a long home run

Fred Hoey in the early 1930s at Fenway Park.

and Fred screamed, 'Homer hit a Foxx!'"

Hoey was fired after 11 seasons as a baseball voice in 1936, because his sponsors felt he failed to keep up a steady flow of chatter during the games, thus allowing too many pauses. The Yankee Network claimed no responsibility for Hoey's firing, signing over the rights to hire and fire announcers to the sponsors. Hundreds of thousands of New England baseball fans, including team owners and players, came to Hoey's support. Even President Franklin D. Roosevelt, who listened to Hoey while sailing off the coast of Maine, rallied to his defense. The bombardment of mail did the trick; General Mills and Socony Oil relented, saying, "Never in the history of radio has support been given to any personality comparable to what was given Fred Hoey."

The end of the line finally came for Hoey after the 1938 season. The mood and character of radio were changing. High-pressure salesmanship and fast-talking commercial readers were what the sponsors wanted, and Hoey was from another era. Former second base great Frankie Frisch was picked to replace Hoey, part of a trend toward ex-players in the broadcast booth.

"I don't know if Fred could be as popular today as he was then," said Moakley, who was still working at WNAC in the late 1960s. "It's altogether different today. In the old days we had our ears and our imaginations and Fred made that ballpark just as big and as little, as green or as brown as he desired. We depended on Fred to tell us why the crowd was hollering and where the ball went. In that era I don't think there was anyone better than Fred Hoey."

Hoey died at the age of 65 in November 1949, accidentally asphyxiated by a leak in a gas oven in his Winthrop, Massachusetts home.

Tom "Red" Manning

 Red Manning: CD 1: Tracks 4-6

Like Hoey in New England, Tom "Red" Manning had amassed a huge following in his native Cleveland. Manning's career spanned 44 years, from 1923 until 1967, and included 29 years as voice of Ohio State football and countless NBC network assignments, including the World Series, the All-Star game, the Olympic games, National Air Races, and even the All-American Soapbox Derby. In fact, in 1936, a runaway racer caromed into the makeshift NBC booth in Akron, sending both Graham McNamee and Manning to the hospital with cracked ribs and several bruises.

Besides sports, Manning's versatility saw him cover several Democratic and Republican conventions, and his beginnings as an announcer actually superceded the advent of radio. He was a corner newsboy in Cleveland in 1916 during World War I. When a ring announcer failed to show up at the nearby Olympic Boxing Arena, Manning was plucked off the street by the promoter to fill in because he had the loudest voice. (He had even won a contest as the loudest newsboy in town at Euclid Beach Park.) The promoter gave him a quarter for his papers and $2 for introducing the boxers.

From there Tom became the "megaphone man" at old League Park, the home of the Indians, which was then called Dunn Field. With his megaphone, which stretched four feet in length, Tom announced the lineups to the press and the batteries to the fans. His voice was described as the second loudest noise in Cleveland, the first being the foghorn off Whiskey Island.

His megaphone duties began during the 1920 season and included the World Series between the Indians and Dodgers, a series that saw Cleveland's Bill Wambsganss complete the only unassisted triple play in World Series history and Elmer Smith hit the first grand slam in series history. A player on that Indians team, Jack Graney, would later become the first player-turned-broadcaster on baseball play-by-play. Manning remained the bell-toned megaphone man for six seasons, joining Rudy Vallee as the two handiest men with a megaphone in the country.

Then came an offer from station WJAY to announce their baseball scores for $3 a day. "It was a great sensation to get there in front of the mike and feel that the audience you were addressing didn't happen to be just a few thousand people in the grandstand. I was talking to the whole world and anyone who would listen," Manning said.

His debut, though, was shaky, as he shouted into the microphone like it was the megaphone, blowing out tubes in the transmitter and putting the station off the air for an hour. "It was a good deal because I didn't have much cash at the time," said Manning. "Soon the Bond Clothing Company became my sponsors and outfitted me with a pair of white flannel pants, a blue coat and a straw hat. I even got a raise, to $5 a day."

In 1928, the new general manager of the Indians, Billy Evans, picked Manning to be the team's first broadcaster on WTAM, offering him one bit of advice: "Don't ever attempt to umpire a game, and you'll get along well." Since Evans had just ended a Hall of Fame umpiring career, Tom heeded his advice. His debut came as a surprise. It was June 26, 1928, and Evans informed Tom before the game that they would broadcast a doubleheader. "Billy was going to do the first game and then hand it off to me," remembered Manning. "But he got so excited he lost his voice and turned it over to me after just seven outs."

Tom Manning (left) about to announce starting lineups. Umpire Brick Owens and Hall of Famers Ty Cobb and Tris Speaker are discussing the ground rules in 1920.

Left: Tom Manning with a portable microphone advertises the Ice Capades while atop a camel during the 1930s.

Right: Future Cleveland sportscasting legend Tom Manning bellows out the starting lineups at League Park in 1920.

The 1929 National Air Races brought Manning network attention. He would go on to broadcast from dirigibles and submarines, covering mine disasters, ship christenings and flood tragedies. He joined Graham McNamee at the 1929 World Series and began a string of 10 straight years as McNamee's NBC co-announcer on the Series and other top sporting events.

Although McNamee was ridiculed by many, Manning was one of his biggest boosters. "He had a brilliant voice, fluent delivery, and was more knowledgeable than people think. Before Graham started doing fights, a million-dollar gate was unheard of. After his first boxing broadcast, the crowds mushroomed and the million-dollar gates began. He was the first major sports announcer and had to take it on the chin from all the petty critics. In those days, one mistake became a critic's headline."

Manning expressed fear and a tightening in his throat en route to the first broadcast of the 1929 Series in Philadelphia, wondering aloud how he could possibly please the millions of fans who would be listening to him that day. "The radio audience doesn't consist of millions,"

McNamee told Manning like a father would console his son. "Instead it's just a humble family eagerly awaiting your every word."

Manning was at the microphone when Babe Ruth called his famous home run shot at Wrigley Field, Chicago, during the 1932 World Series and maintained until his dying day that Ruth indeed called the shot. "The Cubs were tossing orange peels at the Babe to razz him. He picked one up and tossed it to the batboy. Then he stepped out of the box, tipped his cap to the Cubs and told them if Charlie Root put the next pitch over the plate he'd hit it into the center-field bleachers. At the same time he made a gesture to center field. Root's pitch was right down the alley, and the rest is history." And this is the way Manning described the moment on NBC:

"Now Ruth is pointing out towards center field and is yelling at the Cubs bench. Someone has just tossed an orange out on the field and Ruth is kicking it over towards the Cubs dugout. Now he's looking toward the stands, again turning and pointing to center field. Here's the 2-2 pitch. ... RUTH CONNECTS AND THERE IT GOES. THE BALL IS GOING, GOING, GOING, HIGH INTO THE CENTER-FIELD STANDS NEAR THE SCOREBOARD! IT'S A HOME RUN! LISTEN TO THAT CROWD!"

In 1938, Manning was named the outstanding baseball broadcaster of the year in the annual *Sporting News* poll. The paper cited Tom's "uncanny ability to shoot from the hip at a microphone, possessing an eye accustomed to making lightning calculations and equipped with a wide vocabulary that reponds quickly with colorful descriptions." *Variety* called him "fast, accurate, clear, impartial, well-informed without hyping the action."

Although millions have toured the Baseball Hall of Fame in Cooperstown, New York since it opened in 1939, Tom Manning has the distinction of being the first to officially enter its portals, and he backed in at that. "While Judge Landis cut the ribbon, I was holding a microphone, describing the ceremony on NBC, and walking backwards," Manning recalled in a 1967 interview.

In 1956, Manning was honored for his 30 years in broadcasting. A day was proclaimed in his honor, and hundreds of noted celebrities and dignitaries paid him tribute. Said former Clevelander Bob Hope: "I've wondered for 30 years how Tom Manning kept so active. His winter invasions of the West Coast were consistently followed by the big question, 'Who does his hair?' Seriously, the Redhead has done more with a microphone and a gift of gab than just about anyone in the industry. Whatever he's got, he should bottle it and sell it, and I'm the first in line on the buying list."

Wrote *Cleveland Press* sports editor Whitey Lewis in 1956: "Manning has fractured his share of English in his ethereal outbursts; strict grammarians have chewed their cuticles to a frazzle while trying to separate the Manning colloquialisms from the dangling participles. But Tom has made 100 friends for every inverted adverb, and the percentage certainly is in his favor."

Towards the end of his career, Manning commented on how the "thrill is gone from radio." He said it was a business populated by "hucksters, copycats and record spinners." Manning retired in 1967 and two years later, Sept. 4, 1969, just a week before his 70th birthday, died of a heart attack in his sleep. In a tribute from the city council, Manning was called one of the ten most important men in Cleveland history.

Cleveland sandlot baseball commissioner Max Rosenblum at the mike with Tom Manning (right). Manning was the host of the ceremonies, which honored Ty Cobb, Babe Ruth and Tris Speaker in 1941.

TOM MANNING
See Page 2

WJAY

Tom Manning interviews Bob Hope in 1965.

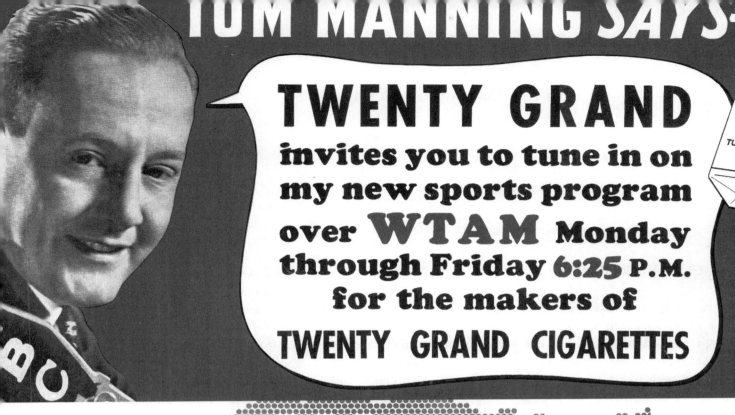

Radio Spot

WTAM — YOUR COMMUNITY STATION

IMMEDIATELY AVAILABLE

on **WTAM**

A new, comprehensive sports-news radio service devoting five minutes to general news and ten to a detailed baseball summary for games, day and night, in all cities regardless of time zone.

**Midnight News and Sports Summary
with Tom Manning**

**12 Midnight — 12:15 a.m.
Mondays thru Saturdays**

Created for a special purpose, this program provides world news coverage followed by a sports resume with Tom Manning. Many listeners depend on morning newscasts for late baseball results due to increased schedule of night contests and difference in time zones. Manning is available with the only complete summary at midnight.

Cost complete, six days, $450 fully commissionable; three days, $275. It is possible to sponsor either news or sports segment alone.

**For details, phone, wire or write Bill Dix,
WTAM Sales Manager, Cleveland 14, Ohio, CHerry 1-0942.**

FRANCE LAUX

 France Laux: CD 1: Tracks 15-17

In 1934, the World Series was sponsored for the first time as the Ford Motor Company paid NBC and CBS $50,000 each for the commercial rights. France Laux was in his third successive year as the CBS broadcaster of the event. His partner was Pat Flanagan, with Tom Manning and Ford Bond handling the play-by-play for NBC.

The year before, Commissioner Landis had relegated the network's two aces, Graham McNamee and Ted Husing, to secondary roles because of their lack of baseball experience. Landis ruled the announcers with an iron fist. He would tell them, "If you see men putting up a gallows in center field and then see them lead me out to it and hang me on it, describe it into the microphone but don't question the justice of the hanging." He was telling the announcers to describe what they saw, without inserting partiality or editorial comment. Landis had rankled over Husing's personal observations during the previous Series, and Husing felt Landis was too restrictive.

Wrote Shirley Povich in *The Sporting News*, "Husing broadcast what he saw, and because he broadcast what he saw, he is penalized." Wrote *Pittsburgh Post-Gazette* sports editor Chilly Doyle about Landis: "Once he gives permission to broadcast, then the broadcasting companies, knowing more about their business and what the fans want than Landis can possibly know, ought to insist on no censorship of any kind."

In St. Louis, no one was more beloved in the 1930s and '40s than Laux. The voice of the Cardinals and Browns had an immense following throughout the Midwest on KMOX radio. Laux was a true pioneer, beginning his radio career on KVOO in Tulsa, Oklahoma, recreating the 1927

World Series. Laux had been working in his own insurance and real estate business in Bristow, Oklahoma when KVOO had an emergency opening for an announcer. Someone had mentioned Laux's name, and station exec Fred Yates tracked him down on a Bristow street, pulling over his car. "'Can you broadcast a baseball game?' Yates hollered. I told him, 'I don't know, but I'll try anything once. Why?'" Laux said. "'Don't ask questions,' replied Yates, 'Just jump in.'"

With all of 90 seconds to prepare, Laux sat down at the KVOO studios, and "what transpired over the next three hours was probably the greatest thing that ever happened to me." He got through the broadcast, and the reviews were positive. Soon came an offer to broadcast Oklahoma and Tulsa college football, and then in 1929, an offer to join KMOX in St. Louis.

"My color man on those early football broadcasts in Oklahoma was George Goodale, who worked as Gene Autry's public relations man for decades. We did our first game from a Model T parked near the sidelines and then used an orange crate and folding chairs. That worked for about a quarter, when a punt returner was creamed by two defenders who landed on the orange crate, smashing it and sending the equipment, the notes and the engineer in three different directions." Speaking of Gene Autry, Laux was the first to introduce the singing cowboy on radio. "It was KVOO and Gene was working as a telegraph operator in Chelsea, Oklahoma," remembered Laux. "Will Rogers had told him he ought to try singing on radio."

Laux joined KMOX for a 30-day trial on March 3, 1929. He was still there 40 years later. Almost from the outset, Laux handled the sports division of KMOX. He began broadcasting Cardinals and Browns games in 1929 and continued for 26 years. "In those early days at

France Laux recreates a game by way of Western Union ticker in 1929.

Sportsman's Park, there was no radio booth. The first two years I sat downstairs in the stands behind the screen and then, to escape inquisitive fans, moved to the edge of the upper deck." There was no such thing as a color man, and during one Sunday doubleheader, Laux was on the air for six straight hours. No other voice was heard on KMOX in that entire stretch.

Laux worked his first CBS World Series in 1933, joined by Fred Hoey of Boston, Roger Baker of Buffalo and Gunnar Wiig of Rochester, with Ted Husing on color. Throughout the 1930s, he was the top CBS voice on the series, working with Jack Graney, Bill Dyer, Boake Carter, Paul Douglas, and, in 1938, a young Mel Allen. All together he did nine World Series and nine All-Star games. His last All-Star game in 1948 in St. Louis was the first one televised. "Only about five or six stations were hooked up to carry the game," said Laux. "Bob Ingham and I worked it. I did the middle three innings and did color on Mutual the rest of the time with Mel Allen and Jim Britt."

When the three New York teams ended their ban on broadcasting in 1939, Laux was the first choice to do the home games of the Yankees and Giants, but he liked St. Louis and turned down the offer because he had become a broadcasting icon in St. Louis. In 1941, he interviewed Stan Musial on his first day in the major leagues and in 1963 he interviewed him before his final game. He broadcast Dizzy Dean's action on the field in his prime and later welcomed him as a broadcast partner. He also took a reserve catcher named Joe Garagiola to his first speaking engagement in 1946 in Peoria, Illinois.

"Joe was shy and timid but was a funny guy who was a natural in front of a crowd," remembered Laux, who did his last season of regular play-by-play baseball in 1948. He did weekend games until the Browns moved to Baltimore in 1954, with regular announcers Buddy Blattner and Dizzy Dean doing weekend telecasts.

Laux stayed active doing freelance work until his death on November 16, 1978 at the age of 81.

Top: *Babe Ruth's final appearance in a big-league ballpark, with France Laux on June 19, 1948.*

Bottom: *Joe Dimaggio, speaking at the same event.*

Left: *Lou Gehrig, France Laux, and Babe Ruth in 1930.*

Right: *France Laux interviews Cardinal manager Gabby Street in 1930. Street later became Harry Caray's partner in the 1940s.*

France Laux store display at Clarks Department store in Tulsa, Oklahoma in 1946.

France Laux, winner of the first Sporting News Announcer of the Year award in 1937.

France Laux, trying to make sense of a Dizzy Dean malaprop in the early 1950s.

France Laux (left) interviewing Pepper Martin, the Wild Horse of the Osage, from the mid-1930s Gas House Gang.

BUDDY BLATTNER

 Buddy Blattner: CD 2: Tracks 30, 32
Dizzy Dean: CD 2: Track 31

Buddy Blattner had quite a career as an athlete and a broadcaster. He was the world table tennis champion for two years in the late 1930s and a major-league baseball player with the Cardinals, Giants and Phillies in the 1940s. With partner Jimmy McClure, Blattner, a St. Louisan by birth, won the world table tennis doubles in 1936 and '37, stunning the favored Hungarians and British.

He began playing professional baseball in 1938, signing with his boyhood team, the Cardinals. Filled with youth and enthusiasm, Blattner absorbed the long all-night bus trips and hot dog and soda pop dinners with ease. He was playing baseball, and the big leagues were his goal. His debut came as a pinch runner in the preseason exhibition between the Cardinals and Browns.

"I almost broke both legs climbing out of the dugout, stumbling, fumbling and falling all over myself in my zest to play. I recalled the Knothole Gang days and how I worshipped the Cardinals and now I was a member of their fraternity. I'll never forget it," remembered the 82-year-old Blattner.

More than three years of military service forced Blattner to start over at the age of 26.

"I witnessed the demise of so many baseball careers which were just coming into blossom when war struck. How I would have done is something that will never be known. I don't weep over it, but it does force me to reflect at times," Blattner said.

Even though he played on the powerful service teams in Bainbridge, Maryland, that were loaded with big league stars, Blattner felt his skills eroding while in the service. It was in the service, however, that he began broadcasting a sports show every evening on the island of Guam. "As a kid in St. Louis, I grew up listening to France Laux, Johnny O'Hara and Gabby Street. Since the service was giving me this opportunity, I didn't complain one bit." He began broadcasting service boxing events and baseball games and after the war spent three seasons with the Giants, ending his career as a 29-year-old player-coach with the 1949 Phillies.

Blattner began his broadcasting career with a televised sports quiz show in St. Louis in 1949. In 1950, he telecast 40 St. Louis Browns games on KDS-TV, the only TV channel in St. Louis at the time. For eight seasons he and Dizzy Dean televised baseball's *Game of the Week*, and there was never a dull moment.

Game of the Week was the first national telecast of baseball on a regular basis. Fans in the Carolinas and the Northwest finally got a chance to see the players they had only heard and read about. "Diz gave no stats," recalled Blattner, "and sometimes he forgot who was playing, but he did a beautiful rendition of 'The Wabash Cannonball.' It didn't make any difference how many mistakes he made, because that's what he was being paid to do. Players returned to their 'respectable' bases, they 'slud' home and were 'throwed' out."

After *Game of the Week*, Blattner broadcast Cardinals baseball, introduced a national television show called *Baseball Corner*, and in 1962, signed to broadcast the games of the expansion Los Angeles Angels. He finished his career as the first voice of the Kansas City Royals in 1969, spending several years in Kansas City before giving way to his partner Denny Mathews, who broadcast his 34th season of Royals baseball in 2002.

Buddy Blattner and Denny Mathews, the first voices of the Kansas City Royals in 1969.

HALSEY HALL

Halsey Hall: CD 2: Tracks 24, 25

In America's heartland in Minnesota, no one was more revered than Halsey Hall, who made his first broadcast in 1922 on WLAS, the forerunner of WCCO in the Twin Cities.

"I was working as a sportswriter on the *St. Paul Dispatch* at the time," remembered Hall, "and I had a 15-minute sports program every Monday night. Then, when Jack Dempsey fought Tom Gibbons in Shelby, Montana, in 1923, I grabbed a megaphone and, from wire reports, stood in the city room of the newspaper and broadcast the fight blow-by-blow to over 2,500 people in the street below."

It was back to writing until 1934 when Hall began announcing University of Minnesota football and Minneapolis Millers baseball. His salary was $5 per game.

Those were the Bernie Bierman years of Minnesota football, and the '34 Gopher team is considered one of the greatest teams ever. The 1970 season marked Hall's 36th straight announcing Gopher football. He also refereed NFL football for 10 years, working many Packers games in the days of the fabled Johnny Blood, Cal Hubbard and coach-quarterback Curley Lambeau. "I worked the last game on the old Green Bay field and the first game in the new stadium, from Lambeau to Lombardi," Hall said.

As far as his broadcasting, with apologies to Harry Caray and Phil Rizzuto, Hall felt he was the first to use the phrase "Holy cow" on the radio. "I first heard it used in 1915 by Billy Sullivan, a very religious man, when I served as Minneapolis Millers batboy. Nineteen years later I began using 'Holy cow' on Millers broadcasts."

His most embarrassing moment in broadcasting occurred in a game against Michigan in Ann Arbor when Wes Fesler was coaching the Gophers. "We were sitting out under a canopy," he recalled, "and when Michigan was teeing up the ball, I still hadn't taken the air. The station was running a commercial. I was ranting and raving, 'For God's sake give me the microphone! To hell with the commercial!' The engineer just shrugged his shoulders, and in the meantime, Michigan kicked off and our halfback, named Engel, ran 98 yards for a touchdown. Then I got my cue. My opening words were, 'Good afternoon, ladies and gentlemen, the Gophers are now lined up for the try for the point after.' The switchboard lit up back at the station and the fans were all upset with me."

Hall, who lent his sparkling wit and half-century of sports experience to the Minnesota Twins broadcasts teamed with Ray Scott, Merle Harmon and Herb Carneal, died on New Year's Eve, 1977, at the age of 79.

Halsey Hall

BILL STERN

 **Bill Stern**: CD 1: Tracks 19-22

"C-O-L-G-A-T-E—Colgate presents Bill Stern, with the Colgate shave cream sports newsreel. Bill Stern the Colgate shave cream man is on the air. Bill Stern the Colgate shave cream man with stories rare. Take his advice and you'll look keen, you'll get a shave that's smooth and clean, you'll be a Colgate brushless fan.

"Good evening ladies and gentlemen, this is Bill Stern, bringing you the 381st edition of the Colgate shave cream sports newsreel, featuring strange and fantastic stories—some legend—some hearsay—but all interesting."

When the popularity, and more importantly, the health of Graham McNamee began to wane in the mid-thirties, a brash kid from Rochester, New York named Bill Stern was picked to replace him. The son of a well-to-do clothing manufacturer, Stern had been a wild youth who was enrolled at the Pennsylvania Military College in 1925. He had been fired from his first radio job just before leaving for PMC, and his first real job after graduation was as an usher at the new Radio City Music Hall in 1930.

Since the studios of NBC were directly across the street from Radio City, Stern constantly plagued program director John F. Royal for a job. Royal decided to let Stern accompany McNamee to a Navy-William and Mary game in Baltimore. Royal thought he would hang himself after a few minutes on the air and then disappear. With two minutes left in a scoreless game and Navy driving, McNamee let Stern take over. To Royal's surprise, Stern sounded good.

He did two more games, and Nick Kenny of the New York *Daily Mirror* wrote: "Stern is interested in what is happening on the gridiron and nothing else, and that's how the radio fans like it. Stern lets the drama of the game itself hold the emotion of the listeners. He loves the game too well

to garnish it with synthetic excitement." Ironically, after Stern had made it to the top, he was accused of being inaccurate and fictionalizing the action on the field.

Royal had come from Cleveland with a reputation for fairness, but he quickly fired Stern when the brash announcer hired an agent to negotiate his contract. Determined to prove Royal wrong, Stern got a job broadcasting games in Louisiana. While driving back from the Texas-Centenary game in 1935, he was involved in a car crash that cost him his left leg. A treatable compound fracture instead became infected because of a doctor's carelessness.

Brought back to New York, Stern was in a state of depression when Royal, hearing about his misfortune, grabbed a breakfast tray from a nurse and entered his room, saying, "How are you going to broadcast next year's football for NBC if you don't eat?" Stern got well and joined the NBC sports team of McNamee, Slater and Don Wilson, who later became famous as Jack Benny's announcer and straight man.

One of Stern's memorable early assignments was the 1939 Rose Bowl, "the most unbelievable game I ever witnessed." Unbeaten and unscored upon throughout the season, Duke was leading 3-0 with two minutes left when Southern Cal inserted a fourth-string quarterback named Doyle Nave and a third-string end named Al Kruegar. Nave tossed four passes to Kruegar, including a 14-yard touchdown with 41 seconds left to give the Trojans a stunning 7-3 win. "For 599 minutes and 19 seconds, Duke had not surrendered a point," remembered Stern, "but they lost the Rose Bowl on the only score they gave up all season."

Stern was a showman and loved to root for the underdog. "I knew if somebody tuned in and I said the score

Bill Stern

was 35-7, they'd tune right out. So I forgot to mention the score and tried to create as much excitement as I could."

Stern's rivalry with Ted Husing and CBS knew no bounds. Minutes before Illinois was to kick off to Army in Champaign, Stern made a dangerous crawl out onto a ledge high above the field and snipped what he thought were the CBS lines. Although one slip would have meant death, Stern could think only of the delight he would experience when Husing was unable to take the air. However, when it came time to go on, Stern received no signal. Scratching his head, he leaned out of his booth and saw Husing begin right on time. He then saw his own engineer scowling. Bill had cut the NBC lines by mistake.

The pain from Stern's car accident forced him to become addicted to morphine and other pain-killing drugs. He wrote about it in his book, *The Taste of Ashes*, and had his life story retold on the *This is Your Life* television program. Amidst his addiction his career flourished. In 1940 he moved into first place ahead of Husing on the *Radio Daily* index of top sports announcers, a position Husing had held for nine straight years. Stern was to hold it for the next 13 years. He did have some good luck physically, too. In 1939, while covering the A.A.U. Track and Field Championships, he walked only a few feet from his metal broadcast booth when it was struck by lightening and destroyed. Another time he survived a train crash that killed 32 people.

In 1952, Stern spent two weeks in the hospital and felt he had kicked his drug habit. He learned, however, that 16 years of drug addiction were not erased in a few weeks. After being told he wouldn't be broadcasting the 1952 schedule on NBC, he turned once again to narcotics. The bubble finally burst at the 1956 Sugar Bowl, when he arrived late and in a stupor and tried to go on with the broadcast. He fumbled and groped for words and finally gave way to partner Ray Scott, who went on to broadcast the game and begin his own renowned career as a radio and television sportscaster. Stern spent six months in rehab and began his comeback in 1957, first as a disc jockey and then in sports at Mutual. By 1958 he had made it all the way back and was voted radio's sportscaster of the year.

Bill Stern's legacy surrounds his *Sports Newsreel* show, which debuted in 1939. Searching for a new twist that would appeal to sports and nonsports fans alike, Stern

concocted yarns involving famous names in history and gave them a sports connection. Armed with a talented group of writers, the show was a smash from the start but ridiculed in the press.

"I've got news for the press," said Stern near the end of his career. "I laughed all the way to the bank. By far the *Colgate Newsreel* was the most popular sports program ever on radio. I wasn't going to change the format to please the press. The show was strictly for entertainment, and we therefore took dramatic license and liberties with the stories. They regarded the program as strictly of a sports nature, and I never did. In fact, I wanted to take the sports out of it completely. The press was basically jealous of radio guys because we made ten times as much money and they felt the announcers didn't know as much about sports as they did, which is probably true."

Among the stories Stern told was one explaining the origin of Thomas A. Edison's deafness. The inventor's hearing problems, according to Stern, came about after he was hit in the head while batting during a baseball game as a youth. The pitcher who beaned him, stated Stern, was Jesse James. (According to Edison's biographers, his hearing troubles began as a youth, when he was soundly boxed on the ears by an irate railroad conductor after causing a mishap on a train.)

"Bill amused me a lot," said the patriarch of New York baseball writers, Dan Daniel, in a 1966 interview. "It was just a question of how much could be believed. On one show Abraham Lincoln was on his deathbed in the boarding house bedroom across from Ford's Theatre after John Wilkes Booth shot him. Just before he died he summoned General Abner Doubleday and whispered to him to invent the game of baseball. Good Lord, no one could believe something like that. I accepted it for what it was, a spoof."

On another *Newsreel* program, Stern told of a girl who played two weeks with the Giants under John McGraw without anyone knowing it. *Atlanta Journal* columnist Ed Danforth wrote: "Bill dares to breathe the warmth of humanity, of curious coincidence and melodramatic setting, into a commonplace incident and leaves his hearers in an emotional glow."

Television forced the demise of the *Sports Newsreel* in 1951 after a 12-year run, as many of Stern's stable of young writers went on to Broadway and Hollywood.

Bill Stern figured in two historic television firsts. On May 17, 1939, he announced the first televised sports event in history as Columbia hosted Princeton in baseball at Baker Field in Manhattan. The game was carried by NBC on an experimental channel, and only one camera was used, which showed the batter, catcher and pitcher. Stern also televised the first college football game, Fordham versus Waynesburg, on September 30, 1939. The game was televised on the experimental W2XBS.

Unlike the majority of sports broadcasters, Stern admitted to me in the twilight of his career that he wouldn't enter the profession if given a second chance. "I think it was the field for me in that I made more money than I could have in another walk of life, but if I had to live my life over, I wouldn't become a sportscaster," he said shortly before his death. "I wouldn't submit myself to the pressures in broadcasting if I could do it again. I haven't faced a microphone yet where I haven't had butterflies in my stomach. I'm glad it's over with, or pretty near over with. I don't know what I'd do, but I wouldn't be a sportscaster."

Bill Stern died of a heart attack at his Rye, New York home on November 19, 1971. He was 64 years old.

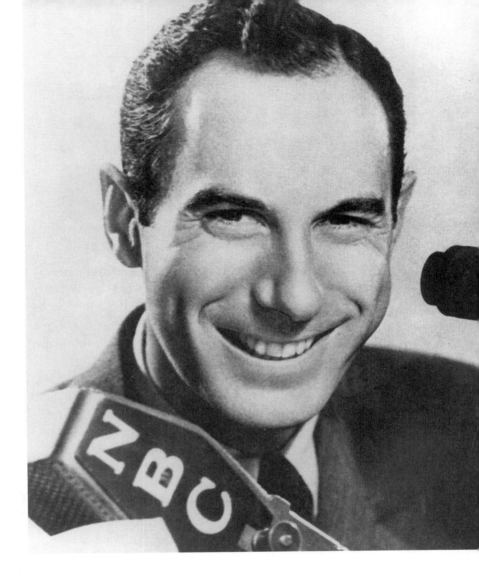

Bill Stern with France Laux in 1955.

123

HARRY WISMER

Ego is certainly part of the broadcasting business, and one of the very biggest egos belonged to Harry Wismer. From radio to executive to one of the founding fathers of the American Football League, Wismer's ego ran out of control. He thought he once owned the world, but at the end he died a lonely, pathetic man.

Growing up in Port Huron, Michigan, in the 1920s, Wismer was a nonstop athlete. Football, baseball, basketball, and tennis occupied most of his time, and when he wasn't playing a sport, he was watching the Detroit Tigers and his hero, Ty Cobb. After graduating from St. John's Military Academy in Delafield, Wisconsin in 1932, he hitchhiked to Florida where he had been recommended to University of Florida football coach Charley Bachman. Wismer made the team, and when Bachman moved to Michigan State to succeed his friend, Jim Crowley, he brought Wismer with him. His football playing days ended when he was carried off on a stretcher during the Michigan game. Coach Bachman, sensing how dejected Wismer was over the injury, persuaded him to try announcing sports on the student radio station, WKAR.

In 1934 Wismer accompanied Bachman to Detroit to watch the Lions, in their first season in the Motor City, play the Philadelphia Eagles. Charley was a guest of the Lions' new owner, G.A. "Dick" Richards, who also owned radio stations WJR in Detroit, WGAR in Cleveland and KMPC in Los Angeles. During the game, Richards complained about the lousy job his P.A. announcer was doing. Soon Wismer was doing the P.A. and working on WJR as the Lions' cub reporter.

Then came a 10-minute nightly sports show on WJR, which involved hitchhiking the 75 miles from East Lansing to Detroit and back to college again. After two years of this, Richards convinced Wismer to give up school and join the radio station full-time as sports director. For six years, from 1935 through 1941, Wismer broadcast the Lions games, when they were led by Dutch Clark, Ace Gutowski, Glenn Presnell, and Bill Shephard, among others.

When Graham McNamee decided to retire from NBC in the early 1940, Wismer was hired as the sports director of the Blue Network, which eventually dissolved and reemerged as ABC. With Bill Stern at NBC and Ted Husing on CBS, the second version of the "Big Three" was established. Wismer built up a vast sports schedule on ABC that included NFL games, the College All-Star game, the Masters and National Open, the baseball All-Star game, and the Sugar Bowl, to name a few. However, new ABC boss Robert Kintner erased them all from the schedule, calling the events nonsense that took up valuable broadcast time. Kintner later took the same tack at NBC, costing the network millions of dollars in revenues before he was fired by David Sarnoff.

Wismer's passion for broadcasting was out of control when he ran ABC sports. Over a 20-year period he broadcast more sports events than all the other network men put together. He traveled more than seven million miles by air. Wismer was a celebrated name-dropper and the last of the Big-Time Operators. "They didn't split Gaul into three parts; he's got it all," said one critic.

Harry Wismer

Wismer began broadcasting Washington Redskins games in 1942. He broadened the network and convinced Amoco oil to sponsor the games. He broadcast the Redskins' fortunes for 15 seasons, clashing often with owner George Preston Marshall in the process. One of their battles concerned Marshall's resistance in signing black players. Their differences got so bad that Wismer sued Marshall in 1957, claiming Marshall was improperly expending funds for his own use. As one writer put it in Wismer's heyday, "Wherever Harry Wismer goes, the dove of peace takes wing."

After helping to found the American Football League and owning the ragtag New York Titans franchise, Wismer saw new life in 1965 in the form of a speedway in his home state of Michigan. His involvement, however, was curtailed because of physical problems. He put off surgery to replace a cancerous hip because he was traveling around ballyhooing the new racetrack. At one point he negotiated a huge contract with the Canteen Corporation of America to help sponsor the track while lying flat on his back. (The track, the Michigan Speedway, became a reality soon after Wismer's death.)

After the hip operation, Wismer had a knee replacement as a result of an old football injury. After months in the Mayo Clinic, he returned to his hometown of Port Huron to convalesce and learn to walk again with the help of crutches. There he was known only as the enthusiastic kid down the block, not the self-centered self-promoter from New York.

"Sitting here all these months has made me realize my mistakes and how much I enjoyed my life in sports," he said in the summer of 1967. "For me, things will never be like they once were, but I'm still young enough to come back. I want to be a broadcaster again."

Five months later, on the night of December 2, 1967, Harry Wismer, back amidst the bright lights of New York City—which he had once left in disgrace, a painful loser after the Titans debacle—collapsed and fell down a flight of stairs in a restaurant-tavern, fracturing his skull. Former friends had turned their backs on him, and he had begun to drink excessively. He was pronounced dead the following morning at the age of 53. This time, the last of the Big-Time Operators was, indeed, gone forever.

Harry Nash, France Laux, and Harry Wismer at the National Open in 1947.

THE WEST COAST

The West Coast was not left out when it came to talented sportscasters in radio's golden age. Among them were Ernie Smith, who for years broadcast the East-West football game, Ken Niles, Jack Keough, Braven Dyer, Bill Henry, Don Wilson, announcer-turned-movie-producer Mike Frankovich, Leo Lassen, Sam Balter, Ken Carpenter, Bob Kelly, Gil Stratton, Keith Jackson, and Chick Hearn, who was the voice of the Lakers in his mid-80s before his passing on August 2, 2002.

Garnett Marks was another big name who began out West. His first experience was as a song plugger for station KFI in Los Angeles, where he later became a staff announcer and baritone singer. Marks moved to KMOX in St. Louis in 1926 and handled baseball and football reporting for the station until 1929, when he returned to Los Angeles to sing in early talking musicals for Warner Brothers and Fox. In 1930 he joined WENR in Chicago, assisting Tris Speaker in broadcasting the games of the Cubs and White Sox. In 1931, Marks, who also used the name Pierce Pennott, returned to St. Louis to assist France Laux on KMOX. Marks moved to WOR in New York in 1934, joined WMCA in 1936, and then faded from the radio scene.

Sam Balter, whose daily sports review, *Sports Book*, was a staple of Southern California radio for many years, was a player, coach, play-by-play announcer, and columnist. He even appeared in movies, as a broadcaster, in *Tom Harmon of Michigan*, *The Pittsburgh Kid*, and *The Jackie Robinson Story*. Born in Detroit, Balter played on the 1936 Olympic basketball team that defeated Canada 19-8 for the gold medal in the sport's first Olympic competition. The game was played outdoors in a torrential downpour which left all 1,500 seats empty. "We went forth to do battle, peering through the darkness of a gloomy twilight at crooked baskets," wrote Balter many years later. "The wind was up, the rain was down, and the spectators were nowhere. Thus began the most important basketball game played up to that time. The world's best players put on a hilarious comedy. A dribble was not a dribble; it was a splash. Players fell and slid. A successful pass was a novelty."

Balter had been a teacher during the Depression in El Segundo, California, but he was disenchanted because teaching offered no rewards for excellence. Salary was based solely on numbers of years one put in. "I could see that a good teacher made no more money, and had no better job, than a bad teacher," he surmised.

Balter's restlessness, combined with listening to a dull sports broadcast of nightly scores, propelled him to sit down at the typewriter and visualize a sports program for radio that would stress heart rather than statistics. His wife suggested the title, *It Happens Once in a Lifetime*. That phrase was to become a household word in sportscasting, as Balter would write more than a thousand stories of strange, great, or paradoxical moments in sports. They were to be heard coast to coast, incorporated into a book, and even released on records. "I took the script to Los Angeles," recalled Balter, "wandered into the local CBS outlet and asked to see the program manager. I knew nobody in radio, had never talked into a microphone. In fact, I'd never even seen one."

Two weeks after dropping off his script, Balter was summoned back to the studio for an air check. A Philadelphia ad man liked the script, and two weeks later Sam was on the CBS-Pacific network. Two months after that, he switched to Mutual, coast to coast, where he made 20 times his teaching salary. He would remain in his new profession for more than 30 years.

Balter became the voice of the Cincinnati Reds in the early 1940s for station WCPO and after one season returned to L.A. where he became the first to telecast Pac-8 football and basketball and Pacific Coast League baseball.

Left: *1993 Cubs-Cardinals game in St. Louis. Charlie Grimm of the Cubs and Jimmy Wilson of the Cardinals are being interviewed by Garnett Marks and France Laux. Gussie Busch, future owner of the Cardinals, is on the left.*

Right: *Sam Balter.*

CELEBRITY BROADCASTERS

Several announcers who gained fame in other arenas cut their eyeteeth on sports broadcasting. Don Wilson, Ken Carpenter, Ed Sullivan, J. C. Flippen, Paul Douglas, Truman Bradley, William Frawley, Joe E. Brown, Marvin Miller, who later starred in the popular TV series *The Millionaire*, and Ronald Reagan all served as sportscasters at some time in their careers. Walter Cronkite announced sports on WKY in Oklahoma City in the mid-1930s. Frawley, who reached the heights as Fred Mertz on *I Love Lucy*, was a great sports fan who served one season as a color commentator on New York Yankee broadcasts.

Philadelphia-born Paul Douglas played pro football with the Frankford Yellow Jackets and semipro Scranton Wasps before embarking on a sportscasting career that would eventually land him in Hollywood. In 1941 Douglas was voted the top sports commentator in the country. Red Barber was picked for play-by-play. Douglas had made his radio debut 13 years before in Philadelphia. He worked as a staff announcer on WCAU before joining CBS as a special events-sports announcer.

Besides studio announcing work on shows like Burns and Allen, Paul Whiteman, Jack Benny and Fred Waring, Douglas also broadcast the World Series and the All-Star game.

In addition to his daily sports column on the air, he narrated sports for the Fox *Movietone News*. Then came the male lead in *Born Yesterday* on Broadway, in which he starred for two years and more than 2,000 performances. The movie version followed, as well as a Hollywood career that saw him play, among many other roles, the manager of the Pittsburgh Pirates in the original 1951 version of the movie *Angels in the Outfield*. Douglas passed away at the age of 52 in September 1959.

The most famous of all ex-sportscasters is of course Ronald Reagan. Nicknamed "Dutch" and raised in the tiny Illinois towns of Tampico and Dixon, Reagan lettered in football, track and swimming at Eureka College. He began his radio career in 1932 with station WOC (World of Chiropractic) in Davenport, Iowa, and became a sportscaster after vividly recreating the last quarter of a college football game while sitting in a studio. Witnesses said the trial broadcast sounded so authentic that when Reagan finished, his clothes were wet with perspiration and he was clinging to the mike for fear of falling out of his chair.

His first assignment was an Iowa football game for $1 and bus fare. He got the job and a 100 percent pay increase. "It was only three more games and $30," recalled Reagan, "but I was a sports announcer. After all, if one buck for playing the game makes you a pro, $10 for talking it should too."

Reagan soon switched to WOC's sister station, WHO in Des Moines, and his radio career blossomed. He specialized in recreating the Chicago Cubs and White Sox games, which were sponsored by General Mills. Reagan had never witnessed a big-league game in person, but with the help of Chicago baseball announcer Pat Flanagan, he quickly mastered the art of telegraphic reconstruction. "Pat was a good teacher, and before too long I was spinning out games for all the world as if I were not 400 miles from the ballpark."

In 1937 Reagan talked the heads of WHO into letting him accompany the Cubs to their spring training camp on Catalina Island near Los Angeles, and it was while visiting Hollywood that he took his now-celebrated screen test.

Sports broadcasting soon gave way to a Warner Brothers movie contract and eventually a political career that ended with the highest office in the country, the presidency of the United States.

Like Ronald Reagan, sports broadcasting served as an early stepping stone for several men who later made their marks in other fields. Ed Sullivan, whose *Toast of the Town* variety show became a staple of Sunday night television for more than 20 years, was a sportswriter in his early days and hosted a nightly sports commentary program in New York. Truman Bradley and J.C. Flippen, both movie actors, were sports announcers before gravitating to Hollywood. Bradley broadcast Cubs games on WBBM, Chicago and was part of the 1935 World Series announcing team.

Comical movie actor Joe E. Brown made several baseball-oriented movies in the '30s and often did guest shots on baseball broadcasts. His son Joe L. Brown was the general manager of the Pittsburgh Pirates for many years. Quiz show host and panelist Bill Cullen did a little bit of everything, including sports, while working on WWSW in his native Pittsburgh in the 1930s.

Towards the end of the 1930s, television began taking the baby steps that would one day see it emerge as a major force. On February 11, 1937, the first large television test took place in Philadelphia with Connie Mack talking baseball with the *Philco Inquiring Reporter*, Boake Carter, at the Philco Radio and Television Corporation. In attendance were nearly 200 editors and publishers of national magazines and newspapers. The respected elder statesman of baseball was interviewed by Carter with the demonstration carried from the Philco factory to the Germantown Cricket Club, miles away, where the guests heard the pair almost as clearly as if they were in the same room.

Babe Ruth led the parade of former players-turned-broadcasters. The Babe, sponsored by Sinclair gasoline, began his program, *Babe Ruth at Bat*, in April 1937. The Bambino mixed personal predictions of current pennant races with recreations of his famous diamond escapades

into a lively twice-a-week 15-minute program.

A former Ruth teammate, Leo Durocher, brought his famous lip to the microphone in 1957, teaming with Lindsey Nelson and Jim Woods on the NBC-TV *Game of the Week* telecasts.

By the mid- to late-1960s ex-players abounded in the booth. Pee Wee Reese, Joe Garagiola, Tony Kubek, Herb Score, Richie Ashburn, Phil Rizzuto, Ralph Kiner, Joe Nuxhall, George Kell, and a host of other former players were permeating the airwaves.

Pat Flanagan and Ronald Reagan.

Comical movie actor Joe E. Brown made several baseball-oriented movies in the 1930s and often did guest shots on baseball broadcasts.

Ed Sullivan, who hosted a nightly sports commentary show in New York.

Philadelphia-born Paul Douglas played pro football before embarking on a sportscasting career that would eventually land him in Hollywood.

Walter Cronkite announced sports on WKY in Oklahoma City in the mid-1930s.

JACK BRICKHOUSE

Jack Brickhouse: CD 1: Tracks 41, 42

At about the same time "Dutch" Reagan was entrenching himself at WHO in the mid-1930s, WMBD in Peoria, Illinois hired Jack Brickhouse to its staff. Six years later Quin Ryan brought him to WGN, thus beginning one of the longest play-by-play careers in baseball history. Starting with radio in 1942 and becoming a pioneer TV baseball broadcaster in 1948, Brickhouse spent 50 years chronicling the Cubs and White Sox in Chicago. He also broadcast Chicago Bears games for more than 20 years.

His approach to sports broadcasting was simple but successful. "I've always tried to keep in mind that I'm in grass-roots country, and I'm grass-roots born and reared. I don't choose to use the so-called sophisticated approach to broadcasting that is used in other parts of the country. I like some 'Gee whiz' and 'Hey, hey' enthusiasm in my broadcasting," Brickhouse said.

The versatile Brickhouse, who commented on courtroom dramas, acted in soap operas, read comics to children and broadcast from airplanes, mine shafts, aircraft carriers and submarines, got his start in radio by entering a local announcers' contest. Brickhouse finished fifth but was offered a job at $17 a week as a part-time announcer and switchboard operator.

"If you worked 80 hours a week in those days, you were loafing," remembered Brickhouse. He did it all, including a tryout as the high school football announcer in Peoria. "I was so bad they had to send a staff announcer out on a streetcar to help me out in the second half. I was going down for the third time when he arrived."

Brickhouse was so despondent he offered to resign, but station owner and pioneer Edgar Bill talked him out of it. When Brickhouse left for WGN six years later, Bill wouldn't let him resign. Instead Brickhouse was on an indefinite leave of absence, with a job waiting if he ever needed it. He never did.

Brickhouse joined WGN in 1940 and became baseball announcer Bob Elson's sports assistant, along with handling the dance band beat, then known as the "milk route." He handled pickups from the Aragon, Trianon, Palmer House, Bismark, Empire Room, Drake Hotel and the Edgewater Beach, working with bands like Guy Lombardo, Artie Shaw and Les Brown, to name a few. Soon he became Kay Kyser's announcer from Chicago's Blackhawk Restaurant.

In Peoria, his only baseball announcing consisted of a few Three-I League games. The first game he worked in Chicago was the second game of a doubleheader at Comiskey Park.

"Elson left early, and I started to do the ninth," said Brickhouse. "But just as I took the air, the plate umpire began waving his hands and players were walking off the field. I had a lump in my throat, my heart was pounding and here the game was being stopped. Even though the sun was still out, I gambled and said the game was called on account of darkness. I was right, as the shadows around the plate area made it tough to see. What a way to break in." When Elson left for navy duty, Brickhouse finished the 1942 season and handled the entire 1943 schedule. This established "Brick" as a full-time sportscaster in Chicago.

After taking off in 1944 for military duty, Brickhouse returned to discover WGN had given up baseball. The Sox games went to WJJD and the Cubs to WIND. Brickhouse left WGN in 1945 to announce the Sox games on WJJD. Elson returned from the navy right before the season and

WGN sportscaster Jack Brickhouse.

Jack Brickhouse (Right) pitching the questions for a baseball quiz May 5, 1941 at Great Lakes Naval Training Center at Fort Sheridan Field House.

supplanted Brickhouse, leaving Jack temporarily unemployed. He quickly got a job in New York, broadcasting the Giants with Steve Ellis on station WMCA, owned by Nathan Strauss, who had a deal with the *New York Times* to broadcast five minutes of news per hour, even during baseball games.

"I was furious," remembers Brickhouse. "The station wouldn't back down, and sure enough, on opening day at the Polo Grounds, the Giants loaded the bases against the Phillies and Mel Ott was at bat, and here I get the signal to return to the studios for news. I refused to give

up the mike, so they took it away from me." The station was bombarded with calls from angry fans, but the *Times* would not give up their policy.

Finally, a deal was worked out with the *Herald Tribune* that permitted suspension of the news during ballgames. "Mr. Strauss was a brilliant man but had very little fondness for sports," recalls Jack. "He loved originating broadcasts of cultural and historical significance but realized once in a while some business had to be transacted with the devil. Thus the baseball games and the revenue it brought."

Jack Brickhouse at the mike.

Strauss was so naive, he once addressed a memo to his station manager that read: "Mr. Stark, I wish you would speak to the managers of the baseball teams and impress upon them the necessity for completing their contests in the prescribed number of innings. Lately, they have used several additional innings in what I must almost consider an attempt to disrupt our program schedule."

Brickhouse returned to Chicago after just one season in New York, just in time to begin telecasting games, of which he became the king. No one has televised more TV baseball than Brickhouse.

Wrote Dave Condon in the *Chicago Tribune*: "They took Jack Brickhouse out of Peoria more than a quarter century ago, but thousands of us cornball baseball fans remain thankful that they've never quite been able to take Peoria out of Brickhouse.

"John Beasley Brickhouse still is the same gee-whiz rube who long ago arrived in this sinful burg to discover for himself if all the things in the mail order catalogs were true. Jack nowadays may be wiser and wealthier, famous and sophisticated and experienced, and yet he continues to approach each baseball game with the mischievous enthusiasm of a kid who has sneaked into the park for the first time." Inducted into the broadcasting wing of the Hall of Fame in 1983, Jack Brickhouse died on August 6, 1998, at the age of 82.

BYRUM SAAM

 Byrum Saam: CD 1: Tracks 37, 38

Philadelphia sported a hallowed roll of top announcers that included Stoney McLinn on WIP, Bill Dyer on WCAU, Joe Tumelty of WFI, and the most legendary of all, Byrum Saam, who began broadcasting Philadelphia baseball in 1938, and 38 years later, in 1975, was still at that post.

The native of Ft. Worth, Texas joined WCCO in Minneapolis in 1936 upon the recommendation of Ted Husing, who had heard him doing TCU football in the days of Sammy Baugh. He announced Minneapolis Millers games in '37 and took a job at KYW in Philadelphia to broadcast football.

Saam's first Philadelphia assignment was the 1937 Temple-Villanova football game. Saam began his long and illustrious baseball career in 1938 as the voice of Connie Mack's Philadelphia A's. He first aired Phillies games in 1939 and until 1950 broadcast just the home games of the Athletics and Phillies.

In the late 1940s, Phillies owner Bob Carpenter insisted on airing the road games too. That meant the Phillies and A's would have separate announcers. Out of loyalty to Connie Mack, Saam became the A's full-time announcer in 1950, and Gene Kelly did the Phillies, who won the National League pennant that year.

When the Athletics moved to Kansas City in 1955, Saam returned to the Phillies, where he stayed until his retirement. When the Phillies won the National League Eastern title in 1976, the Phillies brought Saam back to broadcast the postseason games. He came close to broadcasting his Phillies in the World Series in 1964, but in one of the great collapses, the Phillies blew a 7 1/2 game lead with 12 games left. "We lost 10 in a row," recalled Saam, "with Chico Ruiz of the Reds stealing home to beat us 1-0 in one game and Willie Davis stealing home in the 16th inning to beat us in another, and although Jim Bunning shut out the Reds in the final game of the season, by then it was too late."

During Saam 's 38-year career in Philadelphia, he broadcast more than 8,000 games, 13 no-hitters, including Bunning's perfect game in 1964, Ted Williams's final two games of the 1941 season in which he batted over .400, and two World Series, 1959 and 1965. Saam achieved the highest honor bestowed upon broadcasters when he won the 1990 Ford Frick Award, presented at the Hall of Fame induction ceremonies each year to a deserving broadcaster.

Saam died on January 16, 2000, at the age of 85.

Byrum Saam (middle) broadcasts from Philadelphia in 1939.

STAN LOMAX

 Stan Lomax: CD 1: Track 23

For pure longevity, few can match the career of New York sportscaster Stan Lomax. He began broadcasting in 1930 and was still going strong in the early 1970s, and all on one radio station, WOR. Lomax, along with Ford Frick, who later became commissioner of baseball, was a sportswriter on the *New York American*, which was owned by the Hearst chain. Hearst bought station WGBS, which later became WINS, and dropped the sports reporting duties on Frick and Lomax.

Born in Pittsburgh and raised in Bethlehem, Pennsylvania, Lomax enrolled at Cornell after serving in World War I. He majored in agriculture and intended to be a farmer, but editing the Cornell game programs sent him into sportswriting.

Lomax's first job after graduation was with the *Bronx Home News* in 1923. His first big assignment was covering the memorable Dempsey-Firpo bout at the Polo Grounds in September 1923. "Firpo didn't give a hoot about Dempsey's reputation," remembered Lomax, "and showed great determination and heart. In the first round alone, Dempsey floored Firpo seven times, and the champion was decked twice, the second time falling through the ropes and landing on the typewriter and lap of *Tribune* writer Jack Lawrence. The typewriter was crushed on impact, but Dempsey climbed back in and knocked out the game Firpo in the second round."

Lomax was only two seats behind Lawrence and was awed by what he was witnessing. "People think Dempsey was gladly assisted back into the ring by the writers. Nobody tried to catch Jack when he came through the ropes, and he was assisted only to the point where the writers wanted him off their laps and typewriters."

From the *Home News*, Lomax made the jump to the *Journal* where he covered the Dodgers. His contemporaries read like a Who's Who of great writers: Bill Slocum, Paul Gallico, Damon Runyan, Ring Lardner, Grantland Rice, Roscoe McGowan, Sid Mercer, Dan Daniel and Jimmy Dawson, to name a few. There were 11 writers traveling on the Dodger beat alone.

During the 1930 baseball season, the Dodgers had an off day on the same day as the Yankees. Lomax and his contemporary on the Yankee beat, future commissioner Ford Frick, were both at the paper when Tommy Brooks (head of radio for the Hearst newspapers) walked into the office pointing a finger in their direction. "You fellows are going to be sports announcers!" he exclaimed. Lomax looked at Ford and Ford looked at Lomax. "The hell we are!" they shot back in unison. When Brooks told them there was money to be made, the duo quickly relented. Hearst had just bought WGBS from Gimbels and didn't have much in the way of programming in place. So Brooks went to his pals on the paper to staff the station.

Lomax was one of 11 writers traveling with the second-division Dodgers in the early 1930s. "Soft-spoken Max Carey was manager when I first joined the beat, but things changed in 1934 when Casey Stengel was named manager," said Lomax. "I was lucky enough to be one of 'his writers.' He really took care of us. He never double-talked us like he did with people he didn't know or trust."

After writing his game story, Lomax would scurry off to the radio station to do his sports show. This was difficult on the road, because often the Mutual station was miles from the ballpark. Often he and Frick would recreate games on radio. "Ford was a master at it," said Lomax. "He

Stan Lomax

had such a great imagination. Once he was recreating a game at Wrigley Field against the Giants when a fire nearby the park cut off Western Union contact. Ford didn't miss a beat, having the batter foul off a pitch about eight times and then following with a lengthy argument between the umpires and rival managers. For close to ten minutes, he filled with pure cleverness and imagination."

When the *Journal* merged with the *American* into one newspaper, Lomax left sportswriting to concentrate on radio. By this time Frick had joined the National League as publicity director. The year was 1940. Besides working full-

time on WOR, Lomax freelanced baseball on the Mutual *Game of the Day* as well as the games of the Philadelphia A's, where he worked two years. He also did Army football, Brooklyn Dodger pro football, the basketball Knicks with Marty Glickman, and college games with Don Dunphy in the Garden.

He never missed his nightly show, however, and it became the longest running sports show in history, topping 40 years before Lomax retired in the early 1970s.

Stan Lomax died in 1988 at the age of 89.

Stan Lomax in 1967.

Curt Gowdy interviews Jackie Jenson of the Red Sox in 1961.

THE BIG THREE OF TELEVISION

 Curt Gowdy: CD 2: Tracks 13-15

Curt Gowdy, Chris Schenkel, and Ray Scott all polished their skills on radio and became huge successes on television. Throughout the 1960s and into the 1970s, Gowdy, Scott and Schenkel were the "Big Three" of television. Schenkel, who got his TV start broadcasting the Dumont Network fights, became an ABC fixture on college football, pro basketball, bowling and golf.

His debut in network TV circles occurred when Ted Husing became ill doing the Dumont fights and Schenkel took over. Schenkel idolized Husing, whose full name was Edward Britt Husing. Schenkel named his first son Edward Britt.

A native of Johnstown, Pa., Ray Scott began his broadcasting career on his hometown station after his high school graduation in 1936. He broke into Pittsburgh radio in 1947 as a staff announcer on WCAE, and like Schenkel, got his big network break because of illness to the primary announcer. It was New Year's Day 1956 at the Sugar Bowl in New Orleans between Pitt and Georgia Tech. Scott was supposed to assist Bill Stern, but Stern was confused and in the throes of a drug stupor that saw him break down. The methodical, unflustered Scott stepped into the breach and did a commendable job under trying circumstances. For more than 15 years, Scott televised the games of the then powerful Green Bay Packers and achieved a national reputation for his dramatic, unruffled broadcasts. He also announced the fortunes of the baseball Twins for several seasons.

Curt Gowdy was born in Green River, Wyoming, in 1919 and grew up in Cheyenne, where he was All-State in basketball. At the University of Wyoming he teamed at forward with All-American Kenny Sailors to spark the Cowboys to the Rocky Mountain Conference championship. His first job in sports was on the *Wyoming Eagle* newspaper, and soon there came an offer to work on KFBC in Cheyenne. His first broadcast assignment was a six-man football game in Cheyenne between St. Mary's High and Pine Bluff High on a bitterly cold November afternoon.

"There were no yard markers, no stands and no numbers on the players' uniforms," remembered Gowdy. "There were only about 15 spectators, and since then I've done events that drew over 100,000 fans in the stands, but I never see a big crowd without thinking of those hardy souls who watched that 1943 six-man championship of eastern Wyoming. I never walked into a comfortable, heated booth without thinking of the soapbox at midfield in the freezing playground four blocks from my house. I never see a messenger bringing a hot lunch to a booth without thinking of my little sister Margaret delivering the thermos of soup my mother heated for me. I was hesitant to be introduced by name for that game, because I thought I'd do badly. I wonder what I was ashamed of."

Gowdy's big break occurred when he broadcast the A.A.U. basketball championships in Denver. During the broadcast, Ken Brown, general manager of powerful KOMA in Oklahoma City, was driving through Cheyenne and heard Gowdy's description. Two months later Gowdy got the job of broadcasting Oklahoma football on KOMA, serving as the Sooners' voice from 1945 through 1949.

Gowdy's first coast-to-coast broadcast occurred in 1948 when Oklahoma played Texas Christian in football. The *Game of the Week* was heard over Red Barber's CBS *Roundup*.

While announcing Oklahoma City Texas League baseball games in 1948, Curt was recommended to Mel Allen as a possible partner on the New York Yankee broadcasts.

Curt Gowdy before a Yankees broadcast in 1949.

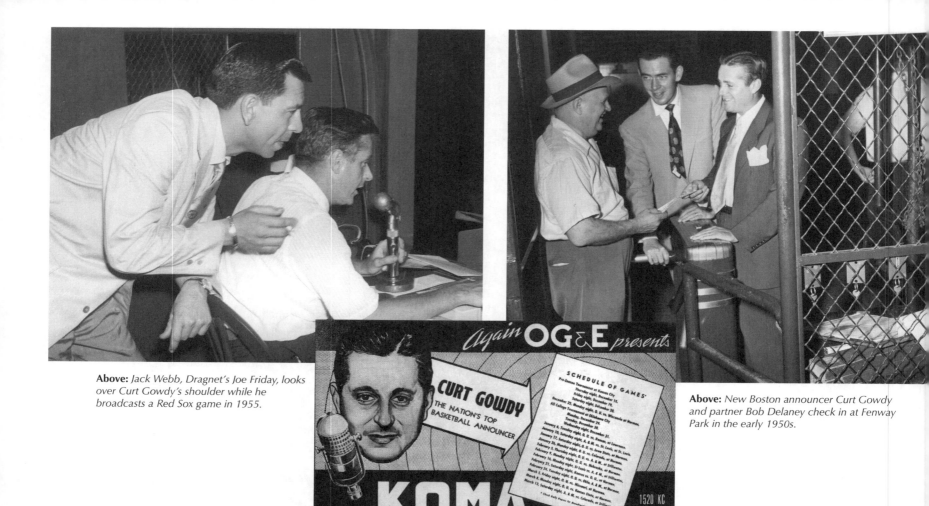

Above: *Jack Webb, Dragnet's Joe Friday, looks over Curt Gowdy's shoulder while he broadcasts a Red Sox game in 1955.*

again OG&E presents

CURT GOWDY
THE NATION'S TOP
BASKETBALL ANNOUNCER

SCHEDULE OF GAMES

KOMA
OKLAHOMA CITY

1520 KC
ON YOUR DIAL

Above: *New Boston announcer Curt Gowdy and partner Bob Delaney check in at Fenway Park in the early 1950s.*

FAN FARE

© Field Enterprises, Inc., 1969

WALT DITZEN

DO YOU REALIZE — YOU'RE STANDING IN FRO OF CURT GOWDY?

8-2

Three hundred applicants were narrowed to three, with Bud Foster of Oakland and Larry Ray from Kansas City as the other two. With Allen and Yankee radio director Trevor Adams in his corner, Gowdy got the job and in 1949 began his big-league broadcasting career.

"I was in awe of Mel Allen, and the big city overwhelmed me," remembered the now retired Gowdy. "I thought I was pretty good in Oklahoma but found out fast that I really wasn't so hot. Mel sharpened me up on baseball and on delivering commercial pitches."

In 1950, Gowdy left New York to become the voice of the Red Sox, where he stayed for 15 seasons before going with the network exclusively. His partners over the years, whom he always chose, were Bob Delaney, Tom Hussey, Bob Murphy, Art Gleeson, Ned Martin, and Mel Parnell.

In 1961, Gowdy began an eight-year association with former pro football quarterback great Paul Christman that developed into one of the finest sportscasting combinations in history.

"We were a natural together," says Gowdy about his late partner. "I don't know if it was better than any other team, but we certainly got a great deal of publicity from it, even though we were broadcasting primarily AFL games. When Paul left to go to CBS in 1968, I really believe he broke up something special. We went together like hand and glove." Then ABC sports boss Roone Arledge felt they were bigger than the league itself, feeling many fans tuned in just to listen to them.

Despite making his mark on television, Gowdy always preferred doing radio. "There's more freedom. If I wanted to talk about the sky or a fat lady in the stands, I could do it. On TV I was just part of a team and was limited by what was on the screen. I think radio is more challenging and harder to do."

Gowdy believes the two toughest jobs in a major-league city are managing the baseball team and announcing the games. "Everybody in town thinks they can manage the team better and everybody in town thinks they can broadcast the games better. The sports announcer has a tough time winning, just like the manager."

Besides his regular duties on NBC, Gowdy also served as host for more than 20 years for the popular *American Sportsman* program on ABC. It was a labor of love

for Gowdy, who is an avid outdoorsman and skilled fisherman. His outdoor segments with the likes of Bing Crosby, Phil Harris, and Ted Williams were classics.

"The biggest thrill I get out of sports," Gowdy said when I assisted him on his daily sportscasts in the early 1970s, "is seeing the great teams and the great athletes perform. It's like watching a champion race horse run. There are many born and many trained, but the majority never quite make it. Great athletic teams pay a price. They give that little extra. The Celtics, with several blacks, whites and a Jewish coach, had it. The Yankee teams I was with and the Packers of the 1960s are other classic examples. They were open to becoming fat-headed and self-contented, but they had a special form of character and pride that refused to let complacency set in."

Koufax, Gowdy and Reese in 1967.

LINDSEY NELSON

 Lindsey Nelson: CD 1: Tracks 43-45

If Gowdy, Schenkel and Scott were the big three of television in the 1960s, Lindsey Nelson wasn't too far behind. And his career encompassed the 1930s through the 1970s, on both radio and television. With sidekick Red Grange as his analyst, Nelson became synonymous with college football on television, while in New York he broadcast the fortunes of the Mets from their rollicking beginnings in 1962 through the 1978 season, with Bob Murphy and Ralph Kiner as his partners each of those years.

A native of Columbia, Tennessee, Nelson went to the University of Tennessee bent on becoming a sportswriter. Those were great days for Vols football under coach Bob Neyland. In Nelson's last three years, they didn't lose a regular season game and went to three straight major bowls.

"In 1939 we shut out all ten of our regular season foes, the last time a major college has accomplished that feat," remembered Nelson late in his career.

It was the voice of Vanderbilt football, Jack Harris, who provided the inspiration for Nelson to go into broadcasting. He loved Harris's broadcasts, and when he got the chance to spot for his idol Bill Stern at the 1939 Tennessee-Alabama game, he jumped at it. He became NBC's spotter in Knoxville, and when the Vols journeyed to Pasadena for the 1940 Rose Bowl, Nelson went with them to spot for Stern.

Stern then invited him to spot the College All-Star game in Chicago, but the game broadcast was cancelled because of a nationwide address by Vice President Henry Wallace.

"I was in Chicago, without funds, which was quite distressing," said Nelson. "I had 50 cents in my pocket, which meant I could either try and find a place to sleep, or else save the half dollar until the next morning and eat breakfast. After much deliberation I bought a copy of the *Chicago Tribune*. It was the thickest paper in town, and I could spread it out on the grass down in Grant Park. I spent the night in the park, had breakfast with the 50 cents and hitchhiked back to Tennessee. Years later I went to the All-Star game and stayed in the Conrad Hilton, which was a whole lot better than Grant Park."

In his senior year at Tennessee, Nelson got his first real taste of sports announcing, doing the color of the Vol football games on station WNOX in Knoxville, assisting Lowell Blanchard. Nelson's timing was impeccable, because soon after graduation he entered the army in an infantry platoon, later serving in combat in North Africa and throughout Europe.

"The experience one derives from serving in a combat unit may overshadow anything else that ever happens in an individual's lifetime," said Nelson decades after the war. "The emotional effects will probably be greater than anything that could ever possibly happen anywhere. A soldier must develop a philosophical approach, a psychic shield, or he doesn't survive."

Upon discharge, Nelson landed back in Knoxville and became the voice of the Vols in 1948. He formed the Vol Network but stayed only two years before going to work for Gordon McLendon on the Liberty Network in Dallas. McLendon, known as the "Old Scotchman," had given Nelson network exposure by airing a Tennessee-Kentucky football game. Soon came a full-time offer to join Liberty, which specialized in recreating major-league baseball games. Nelson's baseball experience at that time consisted of

Lindsey Nelson at the mike of the Liberty Broadcasting System in 1951.

Lindsey Nelson, when he teamed up with Mel Allen on NBC in 1953.

Knoxville Smokies minor-league games, service games in Linz, Austria, with player-manager Harry "The Hat" Walker, Al Brazle, Rex Barney and other big-leaguers, plus Tennessee Vols baseball. Other broadcasters on the Liberty staff included future Dodger announcer Jerry Doggett and Don Wells, who worked with the White Sox and Angels.

They announced two games a day during baseball season and six football games a weekend in the fall, beginning with the Miami Hurricanes on Friday night and ending with the Los Angeles Rams on Sunday afternoon.

"We had baseball running out of our ears," recalled Nelson. "It seems like every waking moment I was saying 'Play ball with the Liberty Broadcasting System.' It was utter heaven for a sports announcer because we did sports. I once announced 60 games in thirty days."

While baseball was recreated, football was done live. "Our recreations were better than our live broadcasts, and this was one of our problems," remembered Nelson. "We could control all of the factors surrounding a game when we recreated, which we couldn't do when we were at the park live."

A crew was sent to record the playing of the national anthem and the public address announcer at each park for the sake of realism. "So when we said, 'And now ladies and gentlemen, at Ebbets Field in Brooklyn, our National Anthem,' it was really that anthem, just not from that particular day. During a game we had four turntables going simultaneously, two with normal crowd noise and two with more excitement. The engineer controlled the crowd noise to meet the situation of the game. We even used the men's room as an echo chamber to make public address announcements," continued Nelson, smiling at the memory. "We could have done a Monday afternoon game from Wrigley Field directly from the park, but with 4,000 fans it could sound kind of dull. Instead we could recreate the same game and crank the crowd up to 30,000 fans."

The FCC required Liberty to announce before and after a game that it was recreated, but they were so realistic the public thought they were live from the park. Wrote Willie Morris in *The New Yorker*, referring to McLendon and the Liberty network and his boyhood in Yazoo City, Mississippi: "His games were rare and remarkable entities, things of beauty. Later, when I came across Thomas Wolfe, I felt I had heard him before, from Shibe Park, Crosley Field, and Yankee Stadium. On those summer afternoons, almost every radio in town was turned to the Old Scotchman, and his rhetoric dominated the place. It hovered in the branches of the trees, bounced off the hills, and came out of car exhausts...he touched our need for a simple and unmitigated eloquence. In Mississippi, I sometimes think now, it was the final flowering of a poetic age."

At its height, the Liberty Broadcasting System numbered 431 stations, but by 1952, after losing its top sponsor and having rights fees boosted, the network went bankrupt. Nelson then received an offer from NBC sports director Tom Gallery to join the network, which he accepted. The first events he did nationally were in golf, including eight straight U.S. Opens.

Nelson patterned his delivery, voice inflection and intonation after his hero, Bill Stern. There was a time in the late 1940s when you could hardly tell the two apart. "Bill had great style, an enthusiastic delivery and as good a voice as I have ever heard," said Nelson. Ironically, after joining NBC as assistant director of sports, Stern had to report to Nelson.

In 1952, Nelson did the Army-Navy game on radio, and on New Year's Day, 1953, he did his first Cotton Bowl, an assignment he held for more than 20 years. He began his college football telecasting career with NBC in 1953, working with Mel Allen. At the 1954 Cotton Bowl, Red Grange did color for the first time with Nelson, thus beginning Nelson's long association with the legendary Illinois running back.

By the early 1960s, Nelson was on so often he was worried about overexposure. In one 1961 stretch, he broadcast the NFL championship game between the Giants and Packers, followed the next day by the Sugar Bowl in New Orleans, followed by the Senior Bowl and the very next day the U.S. Bowl in Washington, D.C. He did seven bowl games that year, and in an effort to slow down, accepted an offer to become the lead broadcaster for the expansion New York Mets baseball team.

"I had had a wonderful ten-year relationship with Tom Gallery and NBC," said Nelson. "Throughout the decade every administrative sports job in New York except ours had changed hands, most of them several times. One night, after about eight years together, Tom asked me what I thought the secret of our longevity could be attributed to. 'That's easy,' I answered. 'In most setups like this you have one guy who is the boss and you have another guy who wants to be the boss. In our case, I wouldn't have your job and I'm not even sure I want mine.'"

The Mets were soon Nelson's primary calling card, and he suffered through seven losing but never dull seasons before the Miracle Mets won the pennant and World Series in 1969.

"When the Mets began, they were received like a team would be in a small town," said Nelson. "New Yorkers endeared themselves to this bunch of aging veterans and fuzzy faced youngsters. Being around Casey Stengel for four years was special. He was funny and colorful, but he knew his baseball. Just because he couldn't remember your name didn't mean he couldn't sit down and give you a lesson about the pickoff play or how to pitch to a certain hitter."

Nelson's most memorable day with the early Mets occurred on May 31, 1964. The Giants won the first game of a doubleheader, 5-3. The second game was tied 6-6 after nine innings. Third announcer Ralph Kiner had left for the studio to do the postgame show, leaving Nelson to do radio and Bob Murphy television. After the 15th inning, the two announcers switched places. In the 23rd inning, approaching midnight, the Giants scored two runs and won 8-6. The 32 innings in the two games were the most ever played in one day. The nightcap lasted seven hours, 23 minutes, the longest time ever for one game.

Mets broadcasters Lindsey Nelson and Ralph Kiner interview Mets Chairman of the Board M. Donald Grant and general manager Johnny Murphy after the Mets victory in the 1969 World Series.

In 1965 Nelson notched another first, hanging 18 stories high above the Houston Astrodome through an entire game. "That was the only game in which I was a ground rule," said Nelson, "because the gondola [suspended at the apex of the dome] I was perched in was in fair territory."

One of the reasons Nelson took the Mets job was that he wanted to get "involved." As a network sportscaster, he never felt he belonged and that he was almost intruding when he did a broadcast.

"I wanted to have a team to root for. I wanted to be able to exercise an emotional interest in what was happening. Well, I certainly got involved with the New York Mets."

Except that when the Mets played the Orioles in the 1969 World Series, Nelson was not assigned to any part of the first two games in Baltimore. "More than that, I wasn't invited. More than that, I wasn't there. It was the network guys who took center stage while the club announcers were offered token appearances in their home parks."

Nelson's big contribution to the series broadcast, since he knew all the players, was doing the locker room celebration after the Mets clinched in game five. "On the monitor in the locker room I saw Cleon Jones catch the fly ball for the final out. I saw the crowd outside go wild. I saw them tossing the turf into the air. Then the door burst open and in came a jubilant gang of ballplayers. I felt champagne being poured onto my head, running down inside my collar. I felt the embrace of the players as I got my cue and introduced the new world champions. It was an incomparable moment. It could never be repeated," he said.

"A man's career in sportscasting, or anything else, is properly measured not in years or longevity but in the miracles of circumstance—the magic moments—that are afforded him. Some come almost instantly and quite by accident. Others come by design and long periods of dedicated effort. But when they come, and they do, they are yours forever."

Nelson died of Parkinson's disease on June 10, 1995, at the age of 76.

ROSEY ROWSWELL

 Rosey Rowswell: CD 1: Tracks 33-34

The 1930s produced a host of announcers who were not known nationally but who were favorites in certain locales. In Pittsburgh, for instance, Albert Kennedy "Rosey" Rowswell was more popular than the players he talked about.

Rowswell was a little pixie who weighed 115 pounds soaking wet yet was a giant figure in Pittsburgh and western Pennsylvania, proudly calling himself "America's most partial baseball broadcaster." Rowswell was a homespun philosopher who had a jargon and lingo all his own.

"He was the Pirates' MVP, the blithe spirit who brought fans into the park despite mediocre performances," wrote Harry Keck in the *Pittsburgh Sun-Telegraph*. "His patter over the airways meant more to the box office than Ralph Kiner's big bat." His most famous saying came when a Pirate hit a home run. Listeners would hear a little tin whistle and the clattering of broken glass as he spurted, "Raise the window, Aunt Minnie, hear she comes. She never made it, right in the old petunia patch."

He first used the phrase in 1938 after a late season Gus Suhr homer. "I just blurted it out and found the fans were repeating it, so I continued to use it," Rowswell said.

"Dipsy doodle" was his way of saying a batter struck out swinging. When fans heard Rowswell scream "FOB," it meant the bases were "full of Bucs." "Doosey marooney" meant an extra-base hit, and "Put 'em on and take 'em off," meant a Pirate double play. Unlike his last broadcast partner, the loquacious Bob Prince, who shook the glass on a garbage can lid to signify Aunt Minnie's window breaking, Rowswell was deliberate in delivery and prone to

silences on the air as he walked around his chair to bring the Pirates luck.

Rowswell made his radio debut in April 1922 when he interviewed manager Bill McKechnie, Honus Wagner, and Max Carey of the Pirates in conjunction with a Red Cross fund drive on KDKA. Pirates owner Barney Dreyfuss disdained radio, feeling it was giving the public something for nothing at the expense of the ticket buyer. One station tried to pirate the Pirates games from a nearby hilltop overlooking Forbes Field, but Dreyfuss squashed the attempt. But by 1936 Dreyfuss was gone and Rowswell began doing recreations of out-of-town games. By 1938 he was broadcasting home games, and attendance jumped from 600,000 fans to more than a million.

He was a Pirates fan first, last and always. In getting instructions from Commissioner Landis before the 1938 World Series between the Yankees and Cubs, Rowswell was confronted by the stern judge, who said to Rowswell, "Why, they tell me there are people living in and around Pittsburgh who don't even know the names of the other seven clubs in the National League!"

Rowswell had a huge following of female listeners as well as shut-ins. There was many a burnt roast or a late dinner blamed on the attention paid to Rowswell's broadcasts.

Once he invited female listeners to come and see him recreate a game in the KDKA studios. Worried that no one would come, he had his wife call a few friends. To Rowswell's amazement, nearly 5,000 women showed up, spilling out of the studio and down several blocks.

Rowswell had over 3,000 shut-ins listed in a file and would dedicate home runs, triples and other Pirate doings to them. Once Rowswell wished a happy 15th birthday to a

The one and only Rosey Rowswell, circa 1940.

young girl stricken with infantile paralysis. A week or so later he received a scrawled letter from the girl, stating that she had received 438 cards and letters, sizeable sums in war savings stamps, candy, cash, jewelry, a radio, and other gifts.

Rowswell was also gifted at composing verse, and his best remembered poem was titled *Should You Go First*, which was born out of a conversation with his wife, Gyp, on what the other would do if one passed away. The final stanza went: "Should you go first and I remain, one thing I'd have you do. Walk slowly down that long, lone path, for soon I'll follow you. I'll want to know each step you take, that I may walk the same. For some day down that lonely road, you'll hear me call your name."

A part owner of the Pirates, legendary crooner Bing Crosby did an occasional guest appearance with Rosey Rowswell, including an April 1948 broadcast:

ROWSWELL: Ralph Kiner will be the first man to face Cub reliever Doyle Lade. Bing, you've been doing a grand job, come right back in here.

BING: You're probably tired of my monotonous patter, but I'd like to see Ralph improve a little off his showing so far this afternoon. He didn't do much off Bob Rush. Maybe he'll do better against Lade. AND HE DOES! THERE GOES A...

ROWSWELL (interrupting): THERE GOES ONE! RAISE THE WINDOW, AUNT MINNIE, THERE IT GOES. CLEAR OUT OVER THE SCOREBOARD...OVER INTO SCHENLEY PARK...HIS FIRST OF THE 1948 SEASON!

BING: WOW, DID HE...

ROWSWELL (interrupting): LET'S HOPE IT'S THE FIRST OF 61.

CROSBY: Ralph is beaming! Ralph is beaming!

ROWSWELL: I just had to take that one, Bing, because we got a little corner on Ralph's home runs.

BING: Well, I'm glad you did, Rosey. Ralph is really beaming. He hit it over the fence, the scoreboard, the clock,

everything. I said that Pafko hit a hard smash here yesterday for the home run. May I tell you something...it was a swinging bunt compared to the one Ralph just hit.

At the end of the game Bing added, "I hope to be back to talk to you over this microphone in May when I'm back in town. I know you'll excuse my deficiencies as a baseball broadcaster, but Rosey seems to think I bring him luck up here, and if I do, I'm only too willing to appear and contribute whatever I can to the color out here at Forbes Field."

In the 18 years that Rowswell was the voice of the Pirates, they never won a World Series or even a pennant. The team was usually mired in the second division.

On February 6, 1955, preparing for his trip to spring training, Rowswell was stricken with a sudden heart attack. He was 71 years old. A fan, Billy Neilan, penned a poetic tribute which read, in part: "At old Forbes Field this season, when the umpire shouts 'play ball,' a voice that is stilled forever will be missed by one and all. The voice of Rosey Rowswell, we will never hear his like, the game will never seem the same, without him at the mike."

Rosey Rowswell blows his dipsy-doodle whistle while young Bob Prince shakes glass and metal to signify a Pirate home run with Aunt Minnie failing to get her window up in time. Circa 1950.

Rosey Rowswell prepares for a game.

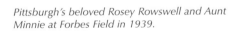

Pittsburgh's beloved Rosey Rowswell and Aunt Minnie at Forbes Field in 1939.

BOB PRINCE

 Bob Prince: CD 1: Tracks 32, 35, 36

Rosey Rowswell's successor in Pittsburgh was equally colorful and flamboyant, and like Rowswell, he lived and died with the Pirates. Bob Prince, who had spent 10 years as Rowswell's assistant, attributed much of his own success to the one and only Rowswell.

Born in Los Angeles in a military family, Prince spent his childhood living on army posts all over the world. He played just about every sport imaginable, with swimming and polo his two most proficient and fencing close to the top. "Growing up, I shot machine guns, pistols, rifles, bow and arrows, rode wild horses in Wild West shows, broke broncs, and played golf and other rich man's games, all of which were subsidized by the United States government," said Prince. Sports were his life, but never once did he think of becoming a sports announcer.

Inadvertently, his mother strengthened his announcing background with a daily activity. "Every day before I left for school, she would place a word under my cereal dish," remembered Prince. "When I came home from school that day, I had to know how to define the word and how to use it properly. This went on for over ten years, which gave me a pretty good command of the language." When he used words like "ubiquitous" in a broadcast, he'd have people scratching their heads, but "I knew mother would be proud."

Every man in Prince's family with the exception of his father, who went to West Point, went to Harvard Law School. This included his grandfather, three uncles, his brother and several cousins. So Prince was not about to break tradition, and off he went to Harvard. He didn't last long, however. One afternoon in 1938, the future barrister

danced with a stripper in a Boston burlesque house as part of a jitterbug contest. "The thing was shown on newsreels all over the country, including Maxwell Field in Alabama, where my father was now stationed," cringed Prince at the memory. "Dad saw the incident and couldn't understand why I'd be on a stage dancing with a stripper instead of attending classes at Harvard. After thinking it over, he decided I should get out of law."

Finding himself out of school and unemployed, he arrived in Pittsburgh one day and looked up a friend who was general manager of a couple of radio stations. Prince asked for an audition, and after doing some staff announcing, he developed his own sports show. About four years later, an old Harvard classmate, Thomas P. Johnson, bought the Pittsburgh Pirates with a group of men that included Bing Crosby and John W. Galbreath. Prince mentioned to Johnson that he'd love to broadcast baseball if the opportunity presented itself, and soon he was joining Rowswell on the Pirates broadcasts.

In his first year with Rowswell, he was never allowed to broadcast even one pitch. He read the commercials and handled the sound effects. The second year, Rowswell let him do an inning. "I resented it at the time, thinking he was denying me an opportunity to get ahead. In reality he was grooming me as his replacement," Prince said.

Handling sound effects meant shaking the garbage can lid filled with broken glass, nuts and bolts that Prince would bounce during Rowswell's home run call of "Raise the window, Aunt Minnie, here it comes." The sound emanating from the hodgepodge in the lid created a terrible racket. Then Rowswell would say, "She never made it. Tripped over a garden hose and broke Aunt Minnie's window."

Bob Prince in 1957.

As the years went by, the rigors of baseball broadcasting began taking their toll on Rowswell, and Prince began playing a more prominent role with the play-by-play broadcast. "It was to the point where I would do four or five innings, and if he was tired, I would just keep going," remembered Prince. "If he wanted to take a nap, I'd carry on a little conversation with him even though he was sound asleep."

The rigors of travel would have been too much for Rowswell, so the Pirates recreated games longer than most teams. It wasn't until after Rowswell's death in 1955 that they started broadcasting away games from the parks.

Prince had no aspirations to broadcast for the networks and was content to broadcast the fortunes of the mostly second-division Pirates. His biggest thrill was describing the 12 perfect innings that Harvey Haddix pitched against the Milwaukee Braves in 1959.

"That was the greatest pitched game in history. There has been nobody past or present that has equaled the job Haddix did that night. There wasn't even a tough play," marveled Prince, who added that it was heartbreaking to see Haddix lose the game on an error in the 13th inning. "That was a tremendous episode of Pirates baseball history. I announced the 9th inning, [his partner] Jim Woods did the 10th, I did the 11th, Jim the 12th, and I blew it in the 13th."

Prince's most satisfying season in baseball was, of course, the 1960 "Impossible Pirates" year, capped by Bill Mazeroski's dramatic home run in the bottom of the 9th inning of the seventh and deciding game of the World Series. The series, however, had its pitfalls for "the Gunner," as Prince was affectionately known in Pittsburgh.

"Mel Allen and I shared the play-by-play duties, with each of us doing four and a half innings. During every one of my segments, the Pirates were behind. Not one thing favorable to the Bucs happened when I was at the mike," Prince said.

Even Maz's home run provided a moment of embarrassment for Prince. "NBC had stated that if one's team was leading at the end of eight innings of the seventh game, that team's announcer would go down to the clubhouse and be ready to interview the world's champions. At the end of eight innings, the Pirates were leading 9-7, so I left the press box," Prince said.

Bob Prince in the early 1950s.

"When I got to the clubhouse, Elroy Face was sitting on a bench praying. 'What's going on?' I asked. 'The Yankees have runners on first and third and one already in. It's 9-8.' The Yankees then tied the game, and NBC told me to get back to the booth in case the game went to extra innings.

"Out of view of the field, I was within 50 feet of the radio booth when a tremendous roar went up from the stands. Perry Smith of NBC shouted at me, 'Get back to the clubhouse, you won it!' I fought through 35,000 people, and when I got to the clubhouse I was immediately pushed up on a stage and handed a microphone. I was now being heard all over the world on radio and seen all over the United States, Canada and Mexico on television. I knew that we had won it, but I didn't know the score and didn't know how we had won it. Nobody told me anything.

"In the process of interviewing various members of the Pirates, I saw Bill Mazeroski standing below me with a bat in his hand. Pulling him up on the platform, I said, 'Bill, how does it feel to be member of the world champion Pirates?' He said 'Great,' and I clapped him on the back, kissed him off and went on to somebody else. In the matter of about seven seconds I had disposed of the hero of the moment without knowing he had hit the homer to win the game. It was the big moment, and I blew it."

On a smaller scale than Rowswell, Prince coined some colorful phrases, such as "how sweet it is," and "we had them all the way." He also discovered "the Green Weenie," a creation of trainer Danny Whelan, who used it to put the hex on opposing players.

"It nearly won the pennant for us in 1966," laughed Prince. "Westinghouse devised a machine to rejuvenate it, and they used their atomic power plant to keep it in a deep freeze when it wasn't being used. Green Weenie bumper stickers began appearing all over the country. Pictures were sent to me from Vietnam where a Green Weenie had been painted on a bomb. One photo came from an Indian fakir in Calcutta, India. He was playing a pipe, and coming out of his wicker basket was a Green Weenie."

No one laughed louder or lived life more to the fullest than the Gunner. The Pirates organization showed their esteem of Prince by including him in their annual team picture, a rare honor for a broadcaster. He was as much of a Pirate wearing his colorful sport coat as the players in their black and gold uniforms.

Prince died on June 10, 1985, at the age of 65.

EDWIN "TY" TYSON

 **Ty Tyson**: CD 1: Track 7, 8

In Detroit, Edwin Lloyd "Ty" Tyson had a following similar to Rosey Rowswell's in Pittsburgh. The "Ty" came from Tyrone, Pa., Tyson's hometown, where he grew up with famed choral and orchestral leader Fred Waring.

After a year at Penn State University and 22 months overseas in the 103 Trench Mortar Battery during World War I, in which he participated in some of the bloodiest battles in the history of warfare, Tyson traveled to Detroit to join boyhood friend Bill Holliday, who had become WWJ's first program manager and announcer. It was the spring of 1922. His first job, after a severe case of mike fright, was broadcasting weather reports. Soon he was reading news, booking acts and introducing dance bands.

"Good afternoon, boys and girls, this is Ty Tyson speaking to you from Navin Field," was first heard on WWJ on April 19, 1927, when Tyson broadcast the first baseball game in Detroit. The Tigers, behind Lil Stoner's pitching, beat Cleveland 8-5. Tigers owner Frank Navin had given Tyson permission to broadcast the games even though he feared it would hurt the gate. The exact opposite happened, and Tyson, with his penchant for accuracy, dry humor and knowledge of the game, became a fan favorite.

As Bob Latshaw wrote in the *Detroit Free Press* in 1966, "By the late 1920s and early 1930s, there wasn't an afternoon the Tigers played that anyone could escape hearing Ty. It was possible for a youngster to leave school, walk a mile home, and never miss a pitch in the game, because every house—but every single house that youngster passed—had its radio tuned to WWJ, Tyson and the ballgame."

Tyson's philosophy was to describe the action and not second-guess manager's decisions, umpire's calls or official scorer's judgments.

In 1934, the Tigers won the American League pennant after a 25-year dry spell. Since Commissioner Landis ruled that the team announcers could not broadcast the series, fearing they would be biased to their teams, Tyson wasn't picked to announce the Series. A groundswell movement sent petitions with more than 600,000 signatures to the networks, and a compromise was reached. Landis allowed him to do all the games on WWJ, independent of the CBS and NBC networks.

In 1935, Tyson was picked by NBC to broadcast the Tigers-Cubs World Series nationally, joining Hal Totten, Tom Manning and Graham McNamee. He was also picked to broadcast the 1936 World Series between the Yankees and Giants. Tyson never did away games live, recreating them instead by breathing action and life into brief bits of information coming over on slips of orange paper supplied by Western Union operator "Mac" McCamic.

In 1934, when rival station WXYZ decided to join WWJ and air the home games, former Tiger hitting star Harry Heilmann was picked as broadcaster. The two announcers competed through the 1942 season, when Tyson retired. He came back to work TV games starting in 1947. In 1951, when sickness forced Heilmann to retire, Tyson returned to radio play-by-play for the first time since 1942 and worked both radio and television for his ailing pal.

In 1953, the man known as the "Tyrone Tradition" retired from WWJ after 31 years. He did some color on Michigan State football and some guest shots on Tiger broadcasts with Ernie Harwell after that.

At 7:45 on a cold Thursday morning, December 12, 1968, Tyson died at the age of 80. An era born in carbon microphones, ticker-tape baseball recreations and crystal receivers died with him.

"Ty" Tyson in 1953.

"Ty" Tyson at mike.

JACK GRANEY

Jack Graney: CD 1: Tracks 25, 26

The very first player turned play-by-play man was Cleveland's Jack Graney. Graney was around as a player in 1920 when the Indians won the world championship from the Brooklyn Dodgers, and he witnessed as a broadcaster in 1948 when the Indians beat the Boston Braves in the Series. He finished his career in 1953, when the Indians were a season away from winning 111 games in a 154-game season, only to be swept four games by the New York Giants in the World Series.

His full name was Jack Gladstone Graney, and he hailed from St. Thomas, Ontario. There he was known as "Glad" Graney, and during his days in the big leagues, whenever he heard a fan from the stands shout, "Hey, Glad," he knew someone from his hometown was in the crowd. For 14 seasons, as a Nap and then an Indian, Graney patrolled left field for the Cleveland ball club. From 1932 until advancing age and the demanding schedule of major-league baseball forced his exit, Graney was *the* voice of the Cleveland Indians. And taking everything into account, there were not many finer anywhere. He was there during the time of Earl Averill, Joe Vosmik and Hal Trosky, through the big years of Bob Feller, Lou Boudreau and Kenny Keltner, and bowed out when Bob Lemon, Early Wynn and Larry Doby were at their peaks.

Possessing a crisp, stirring delivery, Graney was a master at setting a scene, and his enthusiasm packed a sense of built-in drama. His ability to recreate a game from telegraphic codes was beyond reproach. It was sitting in a studio and broadcasting an event that was taking place hundreds of miles away that truly tested an announcer.

Graney perfected recreations into a highly precise art form. He said he had an advantage over broadcasters in other cities because he had played in and was quite familiar with every American League park. When the telegrapher handed him a note saying a ball had just been hit off the scoreboard in Detroit, Graney knew exactly where the spot was located because he had bounced off the same wall numerous times during his playing days.

"Actually I disliked recreations," Graney said in his home in Bowling Green, Missouri in 1968. "It was a dizzy job, and more than once I'd wake up in the middle of the night in nervous fright over what had transpired in the studio the night before. If I mistakenly positioned a runner on third instead of second, or had two runners inadvertently switched around in the order they had scored, I'd get letters."

As a player, Graney was not a star, playing in the shadows of Nap Lajoie, Tris Speaker, Addie Joss, Elmer Smith and others. As the leadoff man he averaged more than 100 walks a year. Graney also carved out several firsts as a player. In 1914 he was the first to bat against a husky young left-hander named Babe Ruth. He was also the first big-leaguer to appear at the plate with a number pinned on his uniform.

He remembered his roomie Ray Chapman and the day he was fatally struck by a pitched ball thrown by submariner Carl Mays at the Polo Grounds. Sitting on the bench, Graney watched the ball collide with Chapman's head and then bounce back to Mays, who threw over to first base. With skull fractures on each side of his head, Chapman didn't have a chance. Several players were so distraught after Chapman's death that they took short leaves of absence. Young Joey Sewell was quickly summoned from New Orleans to play short, and the rookie helped spark the

Jack Graney as an Indian player.

Indians to the pennant and world championship.

Retiring from play after the 1922 season, Graney managed Des Moines in the Western League and then returned to Cleveland to sell Ford automobiles. The great crash of 1929, as it did to thousands of others, "knocked the legs right out from under me," remembered Graney. Nobody was buying cars during the Depression, not even used ones.

Tom Manning had been broadcasting the Indians games since 1928 on WTAM, but after the 1931 season, the radio contract shifted to WHK, and a search began for a new announcer. Ellis C. Vander Pyl was selected as the best of a mediocre crop. The sponsor was not happy with Vander Pyl, however, and threatened to cancel his contract unless a better announcer was found. Indians general manager Billy Evans quickly asked Graney to fill in the breach, knowing Jack was having financial problems due to the stock market crash. Within a few hours, everyone's problems were solved. "Before my first broadcast," remembered Graney, "I was so nervous I almost changed my mind and ran out of the booth."

Broadcasting provided Graney with a new lease on life, and he remained for 22 years as the voice of the Indians. His biggest thrill occurred in 1935 when he was asked by CBS to broadcast the World Series between the Cubs and Tigers. He was asked to do the 1934 Series but was forbidden by commissioner Landis on the grounds he might show partiality since he had played in the American League. Graney wrote Landis a letter clarifying that "my playing days are over. I am now a broadcaster and should be regarded as such."

During the '35 Series, Graney snared a foul ball bare-handed during the broadcast and then watched in amazement a few innings later as Babe Ruth, sitting in the stands, also caught a foul ball, prompting co-announcer France Laux to comment on how the two outfielders were in excellent positions to make the catches.

Graney went through six broadcasting partners over his long career behind the mike. Bud Richmond, Gil Gibbons, Lou Henry, Pinky Hunter, Van Patrick and Jimmy Dudley all worked with Jack, with Dudley succeeding him as top announcer in 1954.

In a June, 1970 edition of the *Cleveland Plain Dealer*, Bob Dolgan wrote about what made Graney great. "When he talked you could smell the resin in the dugouts, feel the clean smack of ball against bat and see the hawkers in the stands. He was a careful reporter and observer. He was short on ego and long on talent. His voice dripped with sincerity and crackled with vitality. He made baseball sound like a sport."

From 1908 until 1953, except for the years between playing and broadcasting, Graney was as much a part of Cleveland baseball as anybody.

"I always tried to give the fans an honest account," he said in reflecting back to his broadcasting days. "It was a tremendous responsibility, and at all times I kept in mind the fact that I was the eyes of the radio audience. It was as if I, an artist, was trying to paint a picture. I never tried to predict or second-guess, even though I had played the game. I just tried to do my best and hope my best was good enough."

All indications were that it was plenty good enough. Graney died on April 20, 1978, at the age of 91.

Jack Graney in his baseball days.

Top Left: *Jack Graney (right) recreating a game by wire in 1940 with co-announcer Pinky Hunter supporting.*

Bottom Left: *Jimmy Dudley (left) and Jack Graney in 1953.*

Bottom Right: *The 1935 World Series broadcast from Wrigley Field included, from left to right, Truman Bradley of WBBM Chicago, Jack Graney of WHK Cleveland and France Laux of KMOX St. Louis.*

JIMMY DUDLEY

 Jimmy Dudley: CD 1: Tracks 27-29

Jimmy Dudley was already a broadcast veteran when he joined Jack Graney in the Indians broadcast booth in 1948, and with his signature greeting of "Hello, baseball fans everywhere," he became a fixture for 20 years. "I used to get more letters addressed simply, 'Hello Baseball Fans Everywhere, Cleveland Ohio,'" said Dudley.

Like many baseball broadcasters—Mel Allen, Red Barber and Lindsey Nelson among them—Dudley hailed from the South. Coming from a family of 13, Dudley was born and raised in Charlottesville, in the Shenandoah Valley of Virginia, and was 22 years old before he journeyed above the Mason-Dixon line. A five-feet, seven-inch tall pulling guard in football at the University of Virginia, Dudley also captained the lacrosse team.

By family decree, he was studying to become a doctor, but a volunteer job to broadcast the Southern Conference boxing tournament on the local Charlottesville station helped change his future course.

"I decided not to go to medical school and concentrated on chemistry although I was secretly entertaining thoughts of going into radio," remembered Dudley. "An ill-fated eight months at a Dupont Chemistry lab had me yearning for radio, and I took a $20-a-week job on the local station where I had started, WCHV." The station was so basic and crude that Jimmy would have to pry open a section of the transmitter with a penknife just to turn on the switch that kept the station on the air.

"I would have to call the fellow out at the tower and we'd have to synchronize our sign-on. When we were ready to sign on, he'd say, 'Okay, shove the knife in.'"

While at WCHV he wrote letters to stations all over the country to try and move up the ladder. Station WOL in

Washington offered him a job as a disc jockey opposite Arthur Godfrey, "so you know how many listeners I had." He wasn't there long before embarking for New York where an executive with WCBS recommended him to a station in Waterbury, Connecticut where he learned to do hockey.

After short stints in Syracuse and Pittsburgh, Dudley landed in Chicago where he would cross paths with Hal Totten, Russ Hodges, and a station manager named Ralph Atlass. Totten took a liking to the young WIND announcer and hired Dudley as his assistant for $10 a game, which was big money in those days.

"Totten was wonderful to me, except he would never let me get on the air," Dudley said. "I did learn a great deal from listening to him, and decades later he'd pick me up on radio as he traveled the country and send me a wire. 'Nice going. You're sounding great,' translated, meaning, 'Don't forget I taught you everything you know.'"

In a year and a half, Dudley had gone from Charlottesville to Chicago, but enlisting in the air force in 1942 put his career on hold. He was shipped overseas as an operations-intelligence officer with the Ninth Photo Recon Squadron, under British command in the China-Burma-India theater. Upon discharge in 1946, Dudley became discouraged because he felt all the bouncing around he did before the war was for naught.

Although WBBM in Chicago offered him a job in news and as a disc jockey, Dudley wanted to do sports and had a desire, for some unknown reason, to come to Cleveland. When he arrived he went immediately to old League Park on Lexington and 66th street and asked for Jack Graney, because that was the only name he could remember. Dudley had planned on asking Graney, who wasn't there, if he needed an assistant.

Jimmy Dudley

Dudley then went downtown and applied for a job at WJW. Russ Hodges recommended him to announce Detroit Lions football, but that was just 12 games in the fall. "WJW station manager Ed Paul asked me if I would like to do hockey, and I said, 'If it pays more than five cents a game, I'll take it.' And that was my first job in Cleveland."

Late in 1947, Dudley broadcast a sandlot baseball championship game from Cleveland's Municipal Stadium, and the new sponsor of the Indians broadcasts told his ad agency, "That's the man I want to broadcast Indians games."

"What about Jack Graney?" asked owner Bill Veeck. "Jack Graney can broadcast with us for as long as he desires," said George Creadon, the new sponsor.

Dudley thus began an association with Jack Graney "that was one of the greatest I have ever known."

What a year to break in as a rookie baseball announcer. 1948 in Cleveland was almost mystical as the Indians won the pennant after beating Boston in a playoff, and then beat the Braves in six games in the World Series as the Tribe drew a record 2,620,627 fans. Lou Boudreau, the player-manager, was named Most Valuable Player and Gene Bearden Pitcher of the Year.

"I was scared to death when the season started, but having Jack next to me meant so much," said Dudley. There were a record 73,163 fans on hand for the opener as Bob Feller toyed with the Browns, winning 4-0. "Fortunately, Jack, a man who played in the big leagues before most of us were born, helped soothe my nervousness by his relaxed professionalism. He was so much fun to work with because of his incomparable background."

Dudley's most memorable moment of the 1948 season was an August doubleheader against the Yankees when just a few percentage points separated the Indians, Athletics and Yankees in the standings, with the Red Sox in fourth place, a distant game and a half behind. Boudreau was out with a sprained ankle, plus his shoulder and arm were aching.

"The Indians were trailing 6-4 in the seventh inning of the first game when they loaded the bases," recalled Dudley. "With a left-handed pinch hitter on deck, the Yankees brought in lefty reliever Joe Page. There were plenty of right-handed hitters on the bench, but seemingly on an impulse, Boudreau took his ailing foot out of a bucket of ice water, grabbed a bat and hobbled up to the plate with the crowd going wild. Lou hit a sharp single up the middle to tie the game, which was eventually won by the Indians 8-6. "I'll never forget Thurmond Tucker, who bore a remarkable resemblance to Joe E. Brown, coming off the bench to run for Boudreau with a grin a mile wide. The Indians won the nightcap 2-1 to sweep. Boudreau was, without question, the most popular Indian of my 20 years in Cleveland. Even more popular than Rocky Colavito. I remember when general manager Hank Greenberg mentioned he might trade Boudreau. Just for even mentioning the thought, he was hung in effigy all over the city of Cleveland."

The first playoff in American League history, between the Indians and Red Sox, was scheduled the day after the last regular season game. There had been no time to set up a network, but Detroit called and wanted to tie into the Indians feed. Then the White Sox called, then the Yankees. "Pretty soon there was a large network of stations taking our broadcast," recalled Dudley. "The Indians won 8-3 as Boudreau homered twice. The Indians returned to Cleveland as champions for the first time in 28 years, when now 63-year-old Jack Graney was the leadoff man in the batting order." The Indians' broadcasters began traveling in 1948, doing every game live and direct, which was a thrill for Graney, because he had never made a road trip as a broadcaster.

Graney retired after the 1953 season, and Dudley worked with several partners: Ed Edwards, Tom Manning, Bob Neal, and Harry Jones. Fired by Indians boss Gabe Paul after the 1967 season, an immensely unpopular move with the fans, Dudley moved on to Seattle, where he did the lone year of the Pilots before the team moved abruptly to Milwaukee late in spring training 1970. Dudley wasn't asked to make the move. After 3,500 major-league broadcasts, he was out of a job.

Abruptly, on the Pilots' last spring training game before they uprooted for Milwaukee, his familiar goodbye: "So long and lotsa good luck, ya heah?" was heard for the last time on a major-league broadcast. He moved to Tucson, the longtime spring training home of the Indians, where he did freelance work. In 1997 he entered the Baseball Hall of Fame as winner of the Ford C. Frick award, emblematic of excellence in baseball broadcasting.

Looking back on his baseball broadcasting career, Dudley recalled a letter he received in Braille from a blind boy in Canada, who signed off by writing, "Remember, Jimmy, you are my eyes. Don't ever let me down." Fortunately for all who listened to him, he never did. Jimmy Dudley died on February 12, 1999 at the age of 89.

Bob Feller (left) and Jimmy Dudley talking baseball at KYW studio in Cleveland.

WAITE HOYT

 Waite Hoyt: CD 2: Track 9

Waite Hoyt pitched for 20 seasons in the major leagues, and none were in the city of Cincinnati. Yet over a span of 24 years, he became a huge success in broadcasting the fortunes of the Cincinnati Reds.

Waite actually made his radio debut in 1927 when he notched a 22-7 record with the powerful Yankees. "We had won the pennant by Labor Day, so we virtually had the month of September off," said Waite, over four decades later. "NBC asked me to drop by WEAF every Monday night for 15 minutes to talk about the Yankees and baseball in general." Waite was on for four straight Mondays and received impressive reviews. After pitching for all three New York teams as well as Connie Mack's Philadelphia A's, Hoyt retired in 1938 with 237 wins against 182 losses.

In the winter of 1937, Waite was part of a daily three-and-a-half-hour program on WMCA in New York entitled *Grandstand and Bandstand*, featuring athletes, actors and actresses. The next year he followed Martin Block's *Make Believe Ballroom* on WNEW with his own 15-minute sports program. Then came stints doing the pre- and postgame shows of the New York teams. He yearned to do play-by-play, but the New York stations were under the misconception that ballplayers lacked the expertise and the vocabulary to broadcast. Waite was pleasant, dignified and glib, but he wasn't even permitted to audition.

Late in 1941, WKRC in Cincinnati approached Waite with a firm play-by-play offer. He accepted on the spot. Two other stations were also carrying Reds games. Sam Balter and Al Stephens were heard on WSAI and Roger Baker and Dick Bray were on WLW.

One of Waite's first obstacles was learning how to score a game. "Even though I had played in the majors for 20 seasons, I had never learned to keep score, so I invented a system of my own," he said.

With his casual, sincere, matter-of-fact style, Waite became a tremendous favorite with the fans in the Cincinnati area. His years of playing with Babe Ruth, Lou Gehrig and other greats gave him a wealth of anecdotal material to draw upon. Listeners used to pray for rain so that he would have the opportunity to reminisce about days gone by. Other broadcasters would return to the studio for recorded music or news updates during rain delays, but Waite would entrance the listeners with memories of baseball's golden age.

The first to do a simulcast, reporting a game on both radio and television in 1952, Waite was the last of the major-league announcers to abandon the telegraphic recreations of road games. He retired in 1965 after 24 years and 4,000 games. "Waite Hoyt Day" was held in his honor on Sunday, September 5, 1965. On February 2, 1969, Waite Hoyt was elected to baseball's Hall of Fame. He died in Cincinnati on August 25, 1985, at the age of 85.

Waite Hoyt at the microphone announcing a war bond sales promotion in 1942.

Waite Hoyt, voice of the Reds.

ERNIE HARWELL

 Ernie Harwell: CD 2: Tracks 41-45

Ernie Harwell, who has broadcast major-league baseball in seven different decades, is the only major-league announcer ever traded to a big-league club. Beginning in radio on WSB in Atlanta in 1940, Harwell spent four years as a U.S. Marine during which he was an overseas correspondent for the U.S. Marine publication *Leatherneck*. Upon his discharge he began his long baseball broadcasting career in 1946 with the Atlanta Crackers.

Midway through the 1948 season, Dodgers owner Branch Rickey sent for Harwell, as Red Barber was stricken with an ulcer and the Dodgers were in desperate need of an announcer. Crackers owner Earl Mann, reluctant to part with Harwell, asked for a player in return at season's end. The player was catcher Cliff Dapper, who became the Atlanta field manager.

Harwell remained in Brooklyn through 1949 before joining the Giants in 1950 and teaming with Russ Hodges. In 1954 he became the first announcer of the Baltimore Orioles, who had moved from St. Louis. He departed for Detroit, where he became as familiar in the Motor City as General Motors, in 1960. Harwell has remained in Detroit ever since, surviving a bump in the road in 1992—an ill-conceived coup by Tigers general manager Bo Schembechler, who removed Harwell from the broadcasts in an attempt at a youth movement, only to be bombarded with fan and media criticism that resulted in his return the following year. Before the 2002 season began, Harwell announced that it would be his final season, retiring at the age of 84 after more than 60 years in broadcasting.

A graduate of Emory University in Atlanta, Harwell began writing for the *Atlanta Constitution* at the age of 15 and later became a correspondent for *The Sporting News*. Just before World War II he joined WSB where he began broadcasting Atlanta Crackers baseball.

"I felt that announcing Cracker baseball would be the zenith of my career," said Harwell, a native of Washington, Georgia. "Although it was minor league, I didn't look on it as minor in any degrading sense of the word. In 1946, Atlanta had a great club with Ki Ki Cuyler managing and Billy Goodman, Earl McGowan, and Shelby Kinney the top performers. That, to me, was the real pinnacle."

After being rained out of his first two major-league broadcasts, Harwell launched his major-league announcing career on August 4, 1948, when the Dodgers hosted the Cubs. Three years later came one of his top moments, Bobby Thomson's playoff homer against the Dodgers. Harwell was the only telecaster of the game, one of the first sports events ever televised coast to coast.

Having done all sports, Harwell feels baseball commands more sharpness and knowledge than other sports.

"The early day announcer who didn't know a squeeze play from a base on balls can no longer hold a job. Today, to broadcast a big-league game, you must have the knowledge of a sportswriter, the reflexes of a player, the enthusiasm of a fan and the impartiality of an umpire," Harwell said.

"The job is tougher in broadcasting because the members of your audience are so varied. A truck driver, a college professor, a housewife, a 10-year-old boy, a former player and a Broadway star are among your listeners. You must explain the game to the 10-year-old and the housewife without talking down to the former player. You must be

Ernie Harwell helps honor Boston great Ted Williams in 1959.

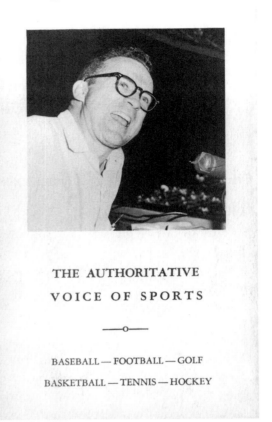

Ernie Harwell

THE AUTHORITATIVE VOICE OF SPORTS

——o——

BASEBALL — FOOTBALL — GOLF
BASKETBALL — TENNIS — HOCKEY

Ernie Harwell (left) and George Kell in 1960.

accurate and colorful enough for the college professor without alienating the truck driver with pontifications. You must show enough inside knowledge to please the ex-player and enough showmanship to keep the Broadway star interested. And nobody will please them all."

Writer, songwriter, inventor and broadcaster Ernie Harwell has come pretty close to pleasing them all for over 60 years.

CHUCK THOMPSON

 Chuck Thompson: CD 2: Tracks 28, 29

Ernie Harwell overlapped with and was succeeded by Chuck Thompson in Baltimore. Broadcasting Orioles baseball and Colts football over several decades, Thompson, with his magnificent voice and pleasing personality, became a legend in Baltimore.

Like many of the earlier announcers, Thompson broke into radio on a dare. "I was a so-called vocalist-front man for Joe Lombardo's local dance band in Reading, Pennsylvania," said Thompson, "and one of the girls in our neighborhood lived next door to the program director of the local radio station, WREW. The girl dared me to audition and even agreed to set the whole thing up. I consented, and after I got halfway through a Moki cough syrup commercial, the program director stopped me and said I'd done enough. I was hired first for part-time but then full-time, for $14.20 a week."

Natives of Palmer, Massachusetts, the Thompson family moved to Reading in 1927. A second-floor boarder at the Thompson home was a Reading Keys player named Johnny Moore, who played in the Phillies and Cubs organizations and later scouted, signing among others Eddie Mathews of the Braves. Young Thompson spent hours talking baseball with Moore, picking his brain on the finer points of the game.

A Carnegie Tech-Albright College football game launched Thompson into sports broadcasting. This was when he joined the Atlantic Refining Co. roster of sportscasters. "My fee was $5 per game, and frankly, I was overpaid," remembered Thompson. "Les Quailey, Ted Husing's partner and head of the Atlantic account for the N.W. Ayer ad agency, worked with me, however, standing outside of the tiny Albright booth, taking notes of my performance, teaching me such tools of the trade as concentrating on down, yardage and team possession over and over again."

Thompson left Reading in 1941 for the big city of Philadelphia and station WIBG, where he remained through 1949 with time out for World War II. On WIBG, he announced baseball, football, basketball, hockey and boxing. His first fightcast originated at the Camden ballpark in Philly between Jersey Joe Walcott and Joey Maxim. "They had a home and home series and their bouts were among the dirtiest I've ever seen: heeling, lacing, thumbing, stepping on each other. Two pros who knew and used all the tricks."

In the 30th Army Division, Thompson saw action in the Battle of the Bulge and returned to WIBG in 1946. Jack Kelly, father of Princess Grace, owned the station and became quite a Thompson fan. Thompson recollected his first major-league broadcast as if it were yesterday.

"In September of 1946, the Phillies and Giants played a doubleheader at Shibe Park and it was 'Radio Announcers Appreciation Day.' By Saam and Claude Haring were honored between games, and I was sent to describe the festivities. This was a pretty big assignment, since there were 26 stations on the Atlantic network," he said.

"I did what I thought was a pretty good job. When the two announcers concluded their thank-yous, Whitey Lockman suddenly stepped into the batter's box to begin the second game. I had never announced a major-league game in my life, but since By and Claude hadn't returned, I had to do something. I suddenly grabbed a scorecard with the lineups and began talking."

Quailey, Saam and Haring all arrived back in the middle of the first inning, and just as the two announcers

Chuck Thompson

177

were about to take over, Quailey stopped them, saying, "No, let him go for awhile." He stopped Thompson after two innings, but the following season the Saam-Haring combo had added a third member—Thompson.

Thompson broadcast his first no-hitter in Philadelphia when Bill McCahan of the A's faced only 28 men in a brilliant performance against Washington on September 3, 1947. "I had learned the meaning of fear while serving in Europe and how it affects different men in different ways. With me, I had difficulty breathing when I became truly frightened, and by the time we reached the seventh inning of McCahan's no-hitter, I was absolutely no use to Saam and Haring in the booth. I was holding onto the railing with both hands, fighting for every breath."

The Orioles were a minor-league franchise when Thompson arrived in Baltimore in 1949 to replace the departing Bill Dyer, who had been quite a crowd favorite with his little red chair that he'd walk around for good luck. Besides broadcasting the Orioles, Thompson also became the voice of the Baltimore Colts.

When the St. Louis Browns moved to Baltimore in 1954, returning the Orioles to the major leagues after an absence of 52 years, Thompson was out of a job since he was working for a rival brewery. After one season on the sidelines, he was back on Orioles baseball in 1955 and 1956 and then went down the road to Washington and helped Arch McDonald and Bob Wolff broadcast Senators games from 1957 to 1961, returning to Baltimore for good in 1962.

Thompson was also a TV regular on NBC's *Game of the Week* in 1959 and 1960 and broadcast his first World Series in 1960. He was part of the national telecasts of Orioles World Series appearances in 1966, 1969, 1970 and 1971. For most of the 1960s and '70s, 17 years to be exact, Thompson teamed with Bill O'Donnell, until Bill's unfortunate passing in 1983.

Unlike some announcers, Thompson was not a ripper. "My philosophy is to report what happens, not why it happens. Our job is not to analyze, our job is to report," he said.

In 1993, the man who created the phrases, "go to war, Miss Agnes," and "ain't the beer cold," became the 17th winner of the Ford C. Frick award for baseball broadcasting excellence at the Baseball Hall of Fame.

Thompson & O'Donnell

SOMETHING SPECIAL

Chuck Thompson tosses out the first ball on opening day. Author Ted Patterson is on bottom left.

Bill O'Donnell smiles approvingly as Chuck Thompson tosses out first ball Opening Day.

There is a great temptation when writing about Chuck Thompson and Bill O'Donnell to start a documentary about their broadcasting accomplishments. And that's easy. It's no problem to say that Bill has done college and pro work in baseball, football and basketball and that Chuck broadcast the famous 1958 Colts-Giants "sudden death" game, the 1960 Yankees-Pirates World Series featuring Bill Mazeroski's classic 7th game homer, four Orioles World Series, etc.

But all that misses the point. Recitations of personal histories and accomplishments are fine, but they do little to transmit to fans the real essence of these two long-time Oriole broadcasters. Perhaps the greatest compliments that can be paid to Chuck and Bill are two words regularly attributed to each by broadcasting personnel, front office staff, players and others with whom they regularly work. They are "pros" and they are "gentlemen."

If these two words seem like faint praise, be assured they are not. Thousands of people all over the country who can talk into microphones call themselves sports-casters. Few can be classified as "professionals" at their craft. Chuck Thompson and Bill O'Donnell work at being accurate, precise and fair to all concerned. That comes across on the air.

"Gentlemen?" Well, let's just say that it's very easy in the glamorous world of professional sports to lose track of who you are and where you've been and to become wrapped up in self-importance. In this world, politeness, good manners and interest in other people and their families can become rare qualities. Chuck and Bill have them.

Are they special? You bet! Just ask anyone who has met them.

JIM WOODS

 **Jim Woods**: CD 2: Tracks 33, 34

Some baseball broadcasters spent decades in the major leagues but were forced to work as number two guys because of more famous partners. Jerry Doggett, Bill O'Donnell, Lon Simmons, Bob Neal, Don Wells, and Jim Woods all fell into that category.

Woods, nicknamed the "Old Possum," worked for six major-league teams and was never the number one guy for any of them. The Kansas City native became the mascot of the Kansas City Blues at age four and the batboy and reader of scores on the local radio station at age eight. As a player, he was offered a Cardinal contract but entered the University of Missouri instead. After six months, at the urging of France Laux and Walt Lochman, he began working on a 100-watt radio station in Mason City, Iowa.

"I was a brash youngster, and my father wasn't happy when I quit college," said Woods. "But I slapped him on the back and left home at 19, saying, 'You'll change your mind the day I walk into Yankee Stadium.' My Dad never lived that long, missing it by two years as he passed away in 1951."

After two years in Mason City, Woods replaced Ronald Reagan, who had left for Hollywood, as the voice of the Iowa Hawkeyes. The year was 1939, and Nile Kinnick and his "Iron Men" were writing a memorable chapter in the annals of college football. "Fourteen men went the entire season," recalls Woods. "Kinnick was their leader. We lost the one game to Tom Harmon and Michigan and won the rest."

Entering the service in 1942, Woods spent four years as a chief petty officer on the Navy War Bond circuit, working with stars such as Farley Granger, Dennis Day and Victor Mature. At war's end in 1946, he joined station WTAD in Quincy, Illinois.

After two years, Woods landed in Atlanta to recreate games for Coca Cola and after just two months replaced Ernie Harwell, who had been called to Brooklyn to fill in for the ailing Red Barber, on Crackers broadcasts. Crackers owner Earl Mann liked Woods and recommended him to Yankees head George Weiss.

"When an opening occurred after the 1952 season, I joined Mel Allen and the Yankees with Joe E. Brown also in the booth. I thought I was pretty good when I joined the Yankees, but Mel soon took that misguided opinion away from me," Woods said.

"In an early exhibition, Mantle was the hitter and I was at the mike. Mel, sitting next to me, had a habit of snapping his fingers when he heard something that displeased him, and after I described Mickey fouling one off back on top, the fingers began to snap. I looked at Mel and said, 'What's wrong?' He looked at me and said, 'On top of what?' 'The roof,' I answered. 'Well, then say the roof and complete your sentence!' Little things like that made better announcers out of all of us who ever worked with Mel Allen."

Woods left the Yankees after the 1956 season and worked with NBC on the *Game of the Week* with Lindsey Nelson and Leo Durocher before joining Russ Hodges with the Giants in their last New York season in 1957. In 1958 he joined Bob Prince in Pittsburgh to help form one of the great teams in big-league broadcasting history. They worked together for 12 years, and "we never had a cross word," remembered Woods. "We had a lot of laughs and a lot of narrow escapes, and it was with a great deal of soul searching that I left Pittsburgh."

Woods joined the Cardinals in 1970. Then came stints with the A's and the Red Sox before hanging up his microphone. His top baseball moment?

"Don Larsen's perfect game in the 1956 World Series. I don't think I've ever been as affected or sat as still as I did the last two innings of that game. I thought to myself, 'Of all the great pitchers who have pitched in the World Series, and here this big goofy so-and-so is going to do it.' My top Pirate thrill was Harvey Haddix's perfect 12 innings against Milwaukee in 1959. It was the most perfect exhibition of pitching that I had ever seen."

Woods received his nickname of "Possum" while with the Yankees. Enos Slaughter had just joined the team, and when the gray-haired, crewcut Woods walked into the clubhouse, Slaughter looked at him and said, "Well, look at that. I've seen better heads on a possum," and the nickname was born.

Jim Woods passed away on February 20, 1988.

A television mobile unit at Wrigley Field on May 8, 1949.

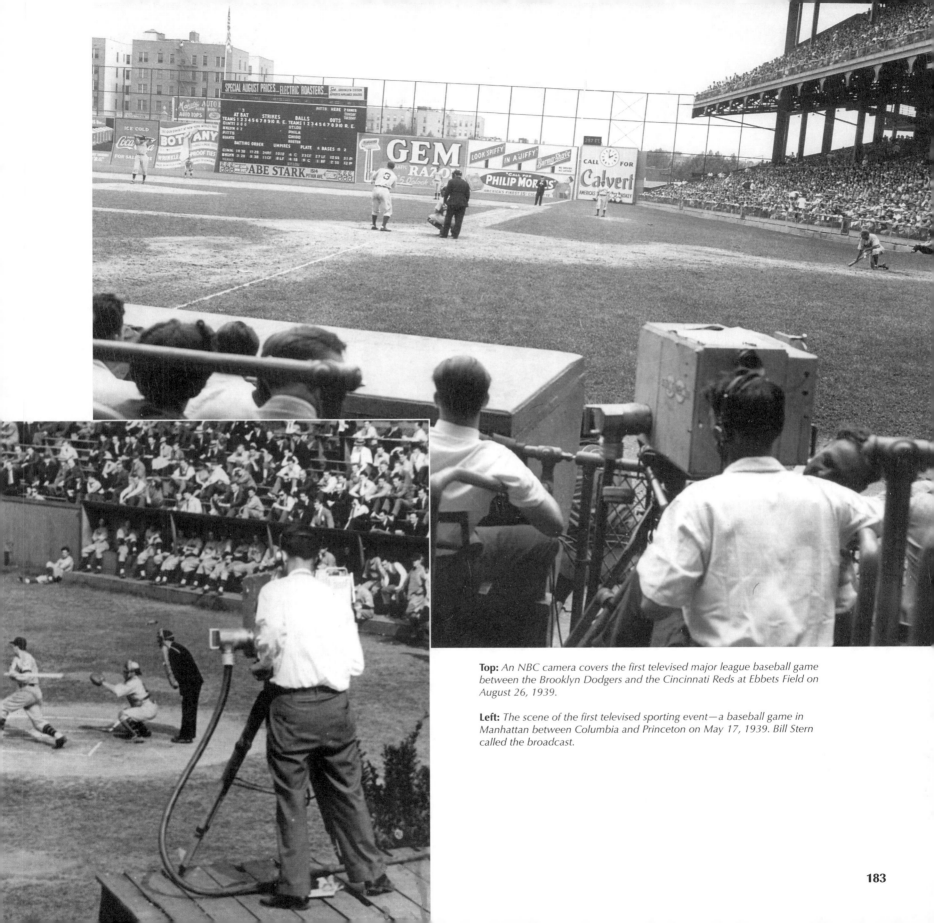

Top: *An NBC camera covers the first televised major league baseball game between the Brooklyn Dodgers and the Cincinnati Reds at Ebbets Field on August 26, 1939.*

Left: *The scene of the first televised sporting event—a baseball game in Manhattan between Columbia and Princeton on May 17, 1939. Bill Stern called the broadcast.*

OTHER EARLY GREATS

A common thread among sportscasters both long ago and into modern times is the lack of security. Knowledge and talent do not necessarily translate into top jobs. A great many of the broadcasters covered in this history were fired at least once in their careers and sometimes more. Not taking it personally is a key to survival.

In the introduction to his book *Careers in Broadcasting*, John H. Leech commented on the "here today, gone tomorrow," nature of the business: "As weary workers in the field will attest, broadcasting creates a pressurized atmosphere in which competitive maneuvers are cutthroat; it affords small opportunity for recognition or distinction among its brainiest professionals; it places your ability and your job on the 'firing line' daily; it promises neither security nor easeful retirement and might unceremoniously discard you after 20 totally demanding years of service, so that you could find yourself high and dry, ulcerous and withered at 45."

The following are some short profiles of other early greats.

Charles "Cy" Casper was one of France Laux's stable of KMOX sportscasters. An all-around athlete at Texas Christian, Casper quarterbacked the Horned Frogs in 1933, when he set a record with a 105-yard kickoff return. Casper played professional football with the St. Louis Gunners, Green Bay Packers and Pittsburgh Pirates, which he quarterbacked in 1935. (Owner Art Rooney didn't adopt the name Steelers until 1940.)

Casper began as a sports announcer at WTSA in San Antonio, covering the games of the Browns' Texas League farm club. Joining the Browns' front office in 1938, he moved to KMOX as a Browns broadcaster, where he teamed with Hall of Fame Brownie George Sisler.

Unlike many sportscasters, Merle Harmon planned on making sportscasting his career from the time he enrolled at the University of Denver after serving in World War II. His first big job was at KJAY in Topeka, Kansas, where his baseball broadcasting debut came with about 30 minutes' notice. The existing baseball announcer had quit suddenly after an argument with the station manager.

"I hadn't even stepped foot in Topeka's ballpark," remembered Harmon. "Topeka was a Class C club playing in the Western Association. After asking directions on where the park was located, I was told the team was out of town. They were playing in Muskogee, Oklahoma, which meant I had to recreate the game over a Western Union wire. That was my baptism under fire."

After four years in Topeka, Merle headed for WHB in Kansas City where he broadcast the final season of the Kansas City Blues. In 1955, he was selected as one of the announcers of the Kansas City Athletics, who moved from Philadelphia after the 1954 season. He made the jump just like a ballplayer, from Class C to Triple A and then the major leagues. Merle broadcast A's baseball for seven years until 1961 when he joined ABC on various assignments. He did the Milwaukee Braves for their final two seasons in Milwaukee, taking over for Earl Gillespie and Blaine Walsh, and then joined the Twins and finished his big-league announcing career with the Milwaukee Brewers.

Cy Casper (left) interviews Al Schacht, a baseball comedian and star pitcher for the Washington Senators, in 1939.

Another versatile early announcer was Bill Slater, a 1924 West Point grad, who taught English and math and was the commandant at a military school in the state of New York before gravitating into radio. While teaching at the Blake school in Minneapolis, a pupil whose father was a radio executive suggested to his dad that Bill would be an excellent choice to announce football. "Like teaching a kid to swim, they just threw me in," said Slater a few years later.

That assignment led to others, including a three-year stint preceding Halsey Hall as the voice of Minnesota football. His first network exposure came in the 1933 Army-Navy game. Slater joined NBC in 1934 and in 1936 was picked to broadcast the Olympic games in Berlin. In 1944 and 1945 he broadcast the World Series for NBC. A versatile performer, Slater emceed several quiz and interview shows including *Breakfast at Sardi's*, which he was hosting when stricken with the leukemia that would prove fatal.

The voice of the Paramount newsreels was at the mike broadcasting a pro football game on December 7, 1941, when one of the most famous bulletins in radio history was issued:

"Jock Sutherland's Dodgers lead the Giants 7-0. Here's the boot. It's a long one ... down to around the three-yard line. Ward Cuff takes it. He's cutting up to his left, over the ten, nice block there by Leemans. Cuff still going. He's up to the 25 and now he's hit and hit hard about the 27-yard line. Bruiser Kinard made the tackle

"WE INTERUPT THIS BROADCAST TO BRING YOU THIS IMPORTANT BULLETIN FROM THE UNITED PRESS. FLASH. WASHINGTON. THE WHITE HOUSE ANNOUNCES A JAPANESE ATTACK ON PEARL HARBOR. STAY TUNED TO WOR FOR FURTHER DEVELOPMENTS WHICH WE WILL BROADCAST IMMEDIATELY AS RECEIVED."

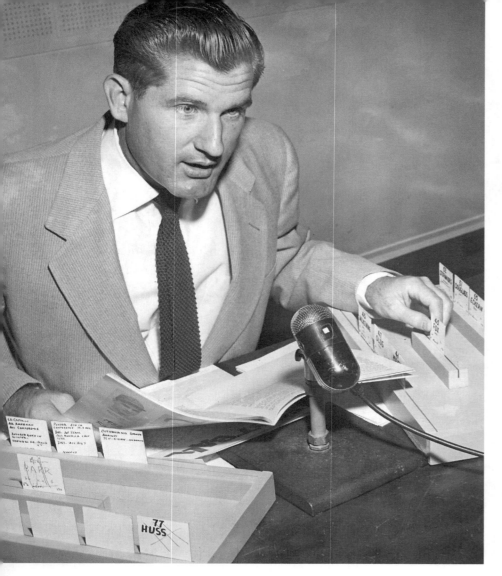

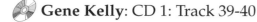

broadcast football beginning in 1939 and in 1964 handled the games of the NFL Cardinals on KMOX in St. Louis. From 1946 through 1949 he joined Bill Slater as the voices of the Indianapolis 500 on Mutual Radio.

Baseball was always his favorite sport to call, and one of his big thrills was describing Carl Erskine's record-setting 14-strikeout performance for the Dodgers against the Yankees in the third game of the 1953 World Series:

"The fans want Erskine to set a new record but you don't get Johnny Mize on strikes very often. The Big Cat is one of the best free swingers in the business. The 0-2 pitch from Erskine—HE STRUCK HIM OUT! CARL ERSKINE HAS SET A NEW ALL-TIME WORLD SERIES RECORD! HE HAS STRUCK OUT 14 MEN, AND TO A MAN, WOMAN AND CHILD, THEY'RE ON THEIR FEET OUT HERE IN FLATBUSH."

Kelly's broadcast philosophy was simple. It consisted of the words, "Once more with feeling, with warmth, with sincerity. The rest is all embellishment, associating certain words with events and plays to make them as clear as possible to the average fan. We try to be truthful and entertaining. We're journalists. Yet we're performers and we want to please the listeners. You can load the air with knowledge and choke the listener to the point he'll lose the impact of the moment. If you care enough to care and are not too thin-skinned, you can make it in this business." Gene Kelly died on September 18, 1979.

Gene Kelly: CD 1: Track 39-40

Versatility was a must for any early radio broadcaster, and one of the most versatile of all the sportscasters was Gene Kelly. At six feet, eight inches tall, Kelly was probably the tallest nonathlete in sportscasting history. His familiar seventh-inning refrain of "Tug on your caps. Rub your noses. Cross your fingers. Up on your feet for the seventh-inning stretch," became a basic staple of his broadcasts of the Phillies and Athletics in the early 1950s. Gene toiled in the bushes, broadcasting minor-league baseball before getting his first shot with the 1950 Whiz Kids as the Phillies won their first pennant in 35 years. In 1962 and '63 he broadcast the fortunes of the Cincinnati Reds. He

Even though he spent most of his career in Ty Tyson's shadow, Harry Heilmann had a huge fan following. Wrote Bill Gilbert, a Tigers fan as a kid, in the June 2, 1969 issue of *Sports Illustrated*, "That he hit .403 in 1923 was not really the impressive thing about the man. The important thing was that Harry Heilmann was God, the Creator, Controller, Communicator of the only universe of importance—Tigerland. He was the mover, the shaker, and the players were his instruments."

Heilmann finished his 15-year playing career with a .342 lifetime average and four batting titles. "He never regarded himself as a great ballplayer or a great

Gene Kelly (right) in 1955. Augie Donatelli is next to Gene. Jim Greengrass is wearing the dark Jacket. Whit Wyatt and Bobby Morgan are on the left.

broadcaster," wrote Detroit sportswriter H.G. Salsinger after Harry's death on July 9, 1951, at the age of 56. "But he was both. His own popularity puzzled him, but it puzzled none who knew him intimately. Few broadcasters in the country ever matched Heilmann in popularity. Few will ever be missed as much."

Heard over station WXYZ, Heilmann began broadcasting Tigers games in 1934. Since he spoke their language, ballplayers confided in him. He had access to information denied to others, and with his personal charm, he helped lure thousands of fans through the turnstiles in both winning and losing years.

Tigers voice Harry Heilmann in 1935.

 Dick Bray: CD 2: Tracks 6-8

In Cincinnati, Dick Bray became a top sports announcer after a 12-year career as a college football and basketball official. For nine years he refereed alongside Frank Lane, who became a controversial baseball scout and general manager. In the 1930s Bray began broadcasting and threw away his whistle to concentrate on radio.

"I believe I'm the only man ever to both officiate and broadcast a game of the stature of Navy-Notre Dame," stated Bray in 1972. He began broadcasting Reds baseball on WKRC in 1934 from a small box on the roof of Crosley Field. Working

with the likes of Red Barber, Roger Baker and Sam Balter, Bray became famous for his 17 years as host of the *Fans in the Stands* program that preceded every Reds Game. With a pack transmitter strapped over his back, Bray conducted more than 35,000 interviews in the show's long run.

How did the show come about? "My Dad and I were listening to the radio the night before the opening game of the 1934 World Series in Detroit, and we heard a special program featuring the comedy team of Olsen and Johnson. Between routines they journeyed to the bleacher ticket line and interviewed some fans. The seed for the new program was planted," he said.

It wasn't until 1938 on WLW that he got the chance to do the program by interviewing fans waiting all night to buy tickets for opening day. Reds owner Powell Crosley also owned the radio station and insisted the program go before each game. When the Reds were out of town and during the winter months, the program originated from a downtown hotel and the Keith's and Albee theatres. *Fans in the Stands* lasted until 1954. Bray stayed in Cincinnati, broadcasting college sports before his retirement. Dick Bray passed away in 1986 at the age of 83.

Wire recreations often provided the chief method of airing out-of-town games. The process was loaded with pitfalls, from wire breakdowns to misinformation. Announcer Bob Eastman worked at KGKB in Tyler, Texas and remembers an incident in 1936.

"One of our young engineers, Billy Smith, was an avid baseball fan and became our play-by-play guy for Texas League games which we received by Western Union ticker. I did commercials and relayed the small coded slips of paper to Billy, who then created the excitement of the game. At one point he motioned for me to cut off his microphone. Apparently on his scorecard he had four men on base. He turned to the Western Union operator and yelled, 'Where the hell is McNabb? I've clean lost the son of a bitch.' Of course when the phones started ringing, it was obvious I had flipped the wrong switch and Billy was very much on the air. Nearly every call was from someone trying to clear up his scorecard."

Leo Lassen in 1965.

Dick Bray does his first baseball broadcast at
Crosley Field in 1935.

The minor leagues, like the majors, sported a host of popular announcers in the 1930s and 1940s. The Wheaties network alone had more than 60 announcers on the payroll, from Art Gleeson in Los Angeles, George Bischoff in Iowa, and Rollie Truitt in Portland to Walt Lochman in Kansas City and Ernie Smith in San Francisco. No one was more popular than Leo Lassen in Seattle.

In 1931, Lassen began broadcasting the games of then Seattle Indians, who became the Raniers. A former newspaperman, Lassen, nicknamed "The Great Gabbo," was known as "Mr. Baseball" in the wilderness of the great northwest, where the closest major-league city was thousands of miles away. His legacy turned to legend. He overcame a rather high-pitched, nasal voice with a love of

baseball, an encyclopedic knowledge of its intricacies and its players, and a swiftness of tongue that put him always on top of the action.

Wrote feature writer Don Duncan in the *Seattle Times* in 1965: "His rather metallic, nasal voice, for which you had to acquire a taste, as you do for green olives, dominated the Seattle scene so completely for so many years that it became part of the family. It was an honest voice, crackling through thousands of screen doors on hot summer nights while sprinklers played on the lawn. You could not escape it, so you listened to the love affair between a bespectacled bachelor and a game called baseball."

This WOR baseball microphone was designed for Mutual's exclusive coverage of the 1939 World Series. Bob Elson and Red Barber broadcast the game.

Epilogue

Regretfully, several talented and capable broadcasters have been given short shrift or omitted altogether from this historical look at sportscasting, not deliberately or with malice, but because of time, space and logistical constraints. Bob Murphy, Gene Elston, Bob Neal, Lowell Passe, Harry Kalas, Dan Daniels, Earl Harper, Lon Simmons, Monte Moore, Claude Sullivan, Van Patrick, Herb Carneal, Bill Dyer, Earl Gillespie, Blaine Walsh, Tony Wakeman, Roger Baker, Marty Brenneman, Denny Matthews, Gerry Gross, Bob Ingham, Al Michaels, Dave Niehaus, Jerry Doggett, Ned Martin, Claude Haring, Tom Cheek, Milo Hamilton, Frank Messer and Don Wells are just a few of that distinguished group.

These men, like all of the broadcasters chronicled in this trip down memory lane, were the pioneers. The pacesetters that preceded wall-to-wall coverage, ESPN *Sportscenter*, and billion-dollar rights packages. They were the versatiles who never met an event they couldn't describe, from an air race to a political convention or a soapbox derby. Another time, another era.

In weaving this tapestry of sports broadcasting's first 60 years, it's evident that there was an emotional bond between announcer and audience that doesn't exist with the same feeling today that it used to. There was a trust and a loyalty that made the broadcaster-listener connection a special one.

There are too many distractions hindering such a relationship today and too much competition for the listener's attention. Broadcasters today, for the most part, lack historical perspective. Superficiality has replaced substance. Television has created "labelers" and not word painters. There are a few exceptions, such as Jon Miller and Bob Costas, who truly love the game, its history, and all the game stands for. Television and its pictures long ago supplanted radio and its words as the top dog of baseball

broadcasting. Yet radio remains the bread and butter medium. Announcers, however, flit from city to city and job to job the same way players do.

In summing up the profession of baseball broadcaster, I'm reminded of the interview I did in Toledo, Ohio, with Connie Desmond, who, despite a losing battle with alcoholism, spoke with eloquence and respect for the privilege of being part of a unique fraternity and a special profession. In our interview he admitted he missed baseball broadcasting.

As Connie so sincerely put it, "When spring training gets under way, the itch becomes almost unbearable. It brings back memories of the breezes of Havana and the Caribbean. And of the great ballplayers. I think of the thrills of the World Series and the All-Star games and the sorrows as well as the thrills. The hours on trains and in the air. The packing, the unpacking. The farewells to your family. Your reception as you walk into a dugout. The faces of men and their ability to rise to the occasion when the odds are against them. It was my job to help report it all to the unseen audience. Everyone struggles through life. Everyone has his highs and lows, and because of the nature of my occupation, I might have had more sorrows resulting from my life than most people would realize. Broadcasting was a demanding occupation, both mentally and physically.

"Just being away from home so long can be heartbreaking. Yet I had to go to the scene; the scene could not come to me. I was fortunate to meet so many great men. The athletes, the coaches, the executives. Men like Branch Rickey, Connie Mack, Ted Husing, Judge Landis and so many more. How would a kid from north Toledo have the opportunity to meet men like that if it wasn't for broadcasting?

"What really is the purpose of a sportscaster? Very simple. We are there because they are not. Those seven words sum up for me the greatest years of my life."

Hear the Voices
Companion Audio; 2 CD Set

Golden Voices Tracks CD 1

1. Introduction by Curt Gowdy (3:22)
2. Harold Arlin broadcast (0:46)
3. Harold Arlin interview (1:41)
4. Tom "Red" Manning interview (1:52)
5. Tom "Red" Manning interview (1:24)
6. Tom "Red" Manning broadcast (0:53)
7. Ty Tyson interview (1:11)
8. Ty Tyson broadcast (1:13)
9. Bob Elson interview (2:56)
10. Bob Elson interview (1:59)
11. Bob Elson broadcast (0:50)
12. Bob Elson broadcast (0:37)
13. Quin Ryan broadcast (1:10)
14. Ted Husing broadcast (0:57)
15. France Laux interview (2:15)
16. France Laux broadcast (1:39)
17. France Laux broadcast (0:37)
18. Pat Flanagan broadcast (1:23)
19. Bill Stern interview (1:44)
20. Bill Stern broadcast (1:32)
21. Bill Stern broadcast (4:01)
22. Bill Stern interview (0:46)
23. Stan Lomax interview (2:02)
24. Mel Allen interview (1:23)
25. Jack Graney interview (1:52)
26. Jack Graney interview (3:04)
27. Jimmy Dudley interview (3:15)
28. Jimmy Dudley broadcast (0:48)
29. Jimmy Dudley broadcast (1:28)
30. Al Helfer interview (3:01)
31. Al Helfer broadcast (1:00)
32. Bob Prince interview (2:14)
33. Rosey Rowswell broadcast (1:35)
34. Rosey Rowswell broadcast (0:28)
35. Bob Prince interview (2:00)
36. Bob Prince broadcast (1:15)
37. Byrum Saam interview (1:20)
38. Byrum Saam broadcast (1:14)
39. Gene Kelly interview (0:39)
40. Gene Kelly broadcast (0:46)
41. Jack Brickhouse interview (2:23)
42. Jack Brickhouse broadcast (0:58)
43. Lindsey Nelson interview (2:45)
44. Lindsey Nelson interview (1:35)
45. Lindsey Nelson broadcast (1:27)

Golden Voices Tracks CD 2

1. Russ Hodges interview (7:06)
2. Russ Hodges broadcast (1:20)
3. Russ Hodges broadcast (0:30)
4. Russ Hodges broadcast (0:56)
5. Russ Hodges broadcast (1:08)
6. Dick Bray interview (1:25)
7. Dick Bray broadcast (1:14)
8. Dick Bray broadcast (0:45)
9. Waite Hoyt interview (2:30)
10. Harry Caray interview (1:44)
11. Harry Caray broadcast (0:54)
12. Jack Buck interview (2:36)
13. Curt Gowdy interview (2:04)
14. Curt Gowdy interview (2:18)
15. Curt Gowdy broadcast (1:18)
16. Vin Scully interview (1:43)
17. Connie Desmond interview (1:40)
18. Vin Scully interview (2:02)
19. Vin Scully broadcast (1:05)
20. Vin Scully broadcast (0:47)
21. Red Barber broadcast (1:15)
22. Red Barber broadcast (0:57)
23. Red Barber broadcast (0:46)
24. Halsey Hall interview (1:31)
25. Halsey Hall broadcast (1:14)
26. Bob Wolff interview (2:59)
27. Bob Wolff broadcast (0:37)
28. Chuck Thompson interview (2:57)
29. Chuck Thompson broadcast (0:48)
30. Buddy Blattner interview (1:35)
31. Dizzy Dean broadcast (0:23)
32. Buddy Blattner/
    Dizzy Dean broadcast (1:05)
33. Jim Woods interview (2:34)
34. Jim Woods broadcast (1:15)
35. Jim Britt interview (2:25)
36. Jim Britt interview (1:09)
37. Jim Britt broadcast (0:34)
38. Vince Lloyd interview (1:24)
39. Vince Lloyd broadcast (0:29)
40. Vince Lloyd broadcast (0:50)
41. Ernie Harwell interview (1:07)
42. Ernie Harwell interview (0:34)
43. Ernie Harwell interview (1:07)
44. Ernie Harwell interview (2:26)
45. Ernie Harwell broadcast (0:45)
46. Connie Desmond interview (2:13)
47. Connie Desmond interview (2:09)
48. Connie Desmond interview (1:11)

CD 1 Sleeve Picture:
Jim Britt and Tom Husing.
CD 2 Sleeve Picture:
Dizzy Dean and Peewee Reese.
CD 1 Picture:
Harold Arlin and Bob Prince.
CD 2 Picture:
Curt Gowdy.

All pictures and audio courtesy of Ted Patterson.